Health Physics

Andrew McCormick

Alexander Elliott

Series editor: David Sang

PUBLISHED BY THE PRESS SYNDICATE OF THE UNIVERSITY OF CAMBRIDGE
The Pitt Building, Trumpington Street, Cambridge, United Kingdom

CAMBRIDGE UNIVERSITY PRESS
The Edinburgh Building, Cambridge CB2 2RU, UK
40 West 20th Street, New York, NY 10011-4211, USA
10 Stamford Road, Oakleigh, VIC 3166, Australia
Ruiz de Alarcón 13, 28014 Madrid, Spain
Dock House, The Waterfront, Cape Town 8001, South Africa

http://www.cambridge.org

© Cambridge University Press 2001

First published 2001

Printed in the United Kingdom at the University Press, Cambridge

Typeface Swift   *System* QuarkXPress®

A catalogue record for this book is available from the British Library

ISBN 0 521 78726 2 paperback

Produced by Gecko Ltd, Bicester, Oxon

Front cover photographs: X-ray and nuclear medicine images of the same
fracture in a human hand, acquired using mobile equipment to avoid
movement of the patient between procedures. The images are digitised
and can be superimposed and co-registered by computer for closer
analysis. Reproduced courtesy of the Department of Nuclear Medicine,
Addenbrooke's Hospital, Cambridge, UK.

Contents

*See the introduction for a note regarding these topics.

Introduction

Cambridge Advanced Sciences

The *Cambridge Advanced Sciences* series has been developed to meet the demands of all the new AS and A level science examinations. In particular, it has been endorsed by OCR as providing complete coverage of their specifications. The AS material is presented as a single text for each of biology, chemistry and physics. Material for the A2 year comprises six books in each subject: one of core material and one for each option. Some material has been drawn from the existing *Cambridge Modular Sciences* books; however, the majority is entirely new.

During the development of this series, the opportunity has been taken to improve the design, and a complete and thorough new writing and editing process has been applied. Much more material is now presented in colour. Although the existing *Cambridge Modular Sciences* texts do cover some of the new specifications, the *Cambridge Advanced Sciences* books cover every OCR learning objective in detail. They are the key to success in the new AS and A level examinations.

OCR is one of the three unitary awarding bodies offering the full range of academic and vocational qualifications in the UK. For full details of the new specifications, please contact OCR:

OCR, 1 Hills Rd, Cambridge CB1 2EU
Tel: 01223 553311

The presentation of units

You will find that the books in this series use a bracketed convention in the presentation of units within tables and on graph axes. For example, ionisation energies of $1000 \, \text{kJ} \, \text{mol}^{-1}$ and $2000 \, \text{kJ} \, \text{mol}^{-1}$ will be represented in this way:

Measurement	Ionisation energy ($kJ \, mol^{-1}$)
1	1000
2	2000

OCR examination papers use the solidus as a convention, thus:

Measurement	Ionisation energy / $kJ \, mol^{-1}$
1	1000
2	2000

Any numbers appearing in brackets with the units, for example $(10^{-5} \, \text{mol} \, \text{dm}^{-3} \, \text{s}^{-1})$, should be treated in exactly the same way as when preceded by the solidus, $/10^{-5} \, \text{mol} \, \text{dm}^{-3} \, \text{s}^{-1}$.

Health Physics – an A2 option text

Health Physics contains everything needed to cover the A2 option module of the same name. This book has been revised and updated from *Health Physics*, previously available in the *Cambridge Modular Sciences* series. There is a colour section beginning on page 21 which is designed to enhance the topics of the eye and colour perception.

It should be noted that chapter 6, 'Diagnostic Nuclear Medicine', and the section on Doppler ultrasonography, in chapter 7, are not part of the OCR Physics A specification. These subjects have been included because the authors and publisher believe they are an important and relevant addition to the specification.

Acknowledgements

24*tl*, Richard Bryant/Arcaid; 24*bl*, Lucinda Lambton/Arcaid; 24*tr,br*, photos by Victoria Hyde; 25, Mark Feinnes/Arcaid; 45, 47*bl*, 53*b*, 69, 70*tr*, 70*br*, courtesy of Siemens Medical Engineering; 47*br*, 48*tl*, *tr*, *bl*, *b*, 49*tr*, *br*, 52*r*, 53*t*, 54*t*, 54*b*, 55*t*, 55*b*, 56, 60*t*, 60*b*, 61, 65*b*, 66*c*, 66*b*, 70*tl*, 71, 76, 77, Professor A T Elliott, Department of Clinical Physics and Bioengineering, University of Glasgow; 65*t*, Simon Fraser/Dept. of Neuroradiology, Newcastle Hospital/Science Photo Library; 72, Nucletron

Every effort has been made to trace and acknowledge copyright but in some cases this has not been possible. Cambridge University Press would welcome any information that would redress this situation.

Body mechanics

By the end of this chapter you should be able to:

1 show an awareness of the *basic bone structure* of the human body in terms of bones, ligaments, tendons, muscles and joints;

2 apply the *principle of moments* and the concept of *mechanical advantage* to bones acting as levers;

3 make a simple analysis of the *forces* involved in standing, bending and lifting;

4 show an awareness of the importance of *correct body posture*, particularly when lifting;

5 describe the magnitudes and directions of forces between the body and the ground when standing, walking and running.

The human body

The study of the human body from a mechanical perspective allows us to analyse techniques for sports and to help prevent injuries to the back or limbs. It also enables informed assistance to those who have sustained back injury, for example, or who suffer from bad posture.

So, here we shall be interested mainly in the muscles and skeleton of the body. Movement of the body involves bones, muscles, ligaments and joints.

Bones

The adult human body has 206 bones. **Bones** are not inanimate structures but living organs that serve several functions. In physical terms they give rigidity and mechanical structure; this is their prime purpose. Bones have a structure of collagen fibres, which have a rubbery nature, and bone mineral. However, bone itself is not very flexible, and the movement of the skeleton is accomplished by **joints**, which are regions where two or more bones come together. The bone surfaces at a joint are covered in cartilage (gristle) and separated from each other by a **synovial cavity** containing a fluid. Where a joint does permit movement, the bones are held together by

ligaments (*figure 1.1*). Joints are classified into four main types, **free-moving**, **slightly movable**, **sliding** and **fixed**, as shown in *figure 1.2*.

Muscles

Muscles are attached to bones by tough elastic **tendons**. There are three different types of muscle; the main one for movement of the skeleton is the voluntary or skeletal muscle. The other two types of

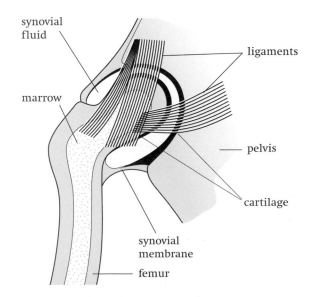

● **Figure 1.1** A hip joint: the ligaments, shown as fine lines, hold the joint together.

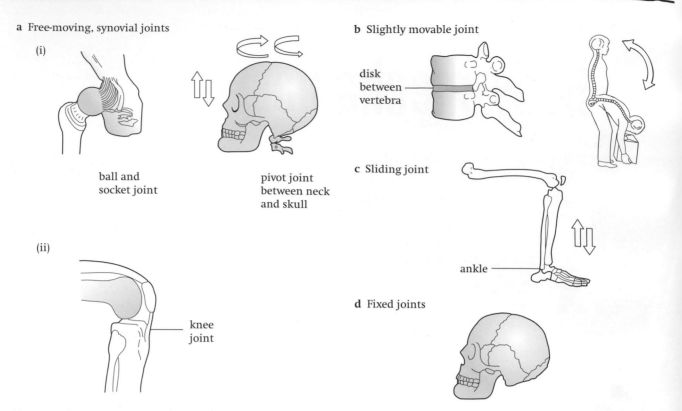

a Free-moving, synovial joints

(i)

ball and
socket joint

pivot joint
between neck
and skull

(ii)

knee
joint

b Slightly movable joint

disk
between
vertebra

c Sliding joint

ankle

d Fixed joints

● **Figure 1.2** Types of joint. **a** Free-moving, synovial joints comprise (i) joints that allow movement in several directions and (ii) joints that allow movement in one direction only. **b** An example of a slightly movable joint is the joint between two vertebrae. **c** The ankle is a sliding joint. **d** The joints of the skull, movable at birth, become fixed joints.

muscle are the involuntary muscles found in the heart and in the blood vessels and alimentary canal. The importance of voluntary muscle is its ability to contract very readily when stimulated.

Muscles can only contract, i.e become shorter and thicker. In doing so, they pull on the bones to which they are attached. When a muscle relaxes, it no longer exerts a pulling force; it returns to its original length. Muscles cannot be lengthened beyond this, so they are incapable of exerting a pushing force. Therefore several muscles are required for the control of a joint with a wide range of movement. Muscles often act in pairs, as at a hinge joint, where one muscle moves the bone one way and another muscle moves the bone the other way. A pair of muscles that have opposite effects is called **antagonistic**; such a pair is the biceps and triceps, which raise and lower the forearm (*figure 1.3*). The muscle that bends or flexes a joint is called a **flexor** and the muscle that straightens or extends a joint is called an **extensor**. *Figure 1.4* shows the muscular action in a runner's legs.

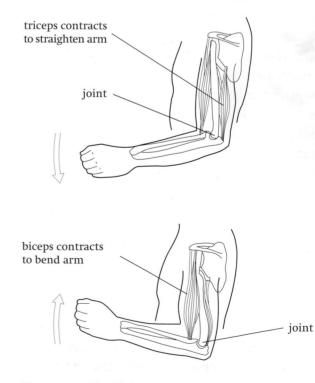

triceps contracts
to straighten arm

joint

biceps contracts
to bend arm

joint

● **Figure 1.3** The biceps and triceps are antagonistic muscles.

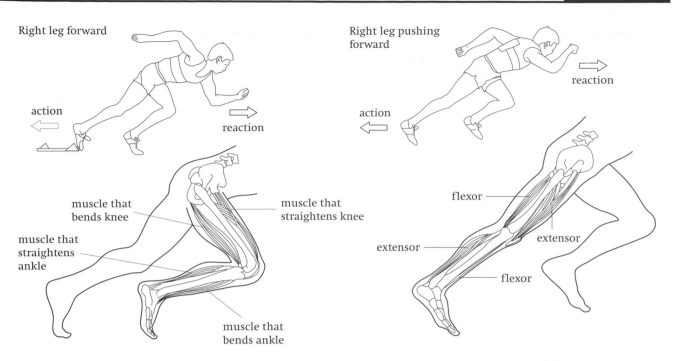

● **Figure 1.4** Flexor and extensor muscles in a runner's legs.

SAQ 1.1

Muscles cannot lengthen yet apparently we use them to push against objects. Explain how the muscles and joint of the elbow allow this to occur. Use *figure 1.3* to help in your answer: imagine that you are starting to push a supermarket trolley, for example.

The human body as a machine

A **machine** is designed to enable a small force to produce a large force (or vice versa) or to enable a force acting at one point to produce a force at another point. A **lever** is one of the simplest machines. The input force, known as the **effort**, is applied at a certain distance from the fulcrum or pivot; the output force or **load** is usually at a different distance from the fulcrum. The **mechanical advantage** (MA) of a lever (or any other machine) is defined as load L divided by effort E:

$$\text{MA} = \frac{\text{load}}{\text{effort}} = \frac{L}{E}$$

Levers found in the human body can be divided into three types, class 1, class 2 and class 3:

■ **Class 1** The fulcrum is between the effort and the load (*figure 1.5a* overleaf). When a cord is pulled the effort (provided by the shortening of the triceps) is actually greater than the load, so the MA is less than 1. Of course, levers in this class commonly have MA values equal to 1 or greater than 1.

■ **Class 2** The load is between the effort and the fulcrum (*figure 1.5b*). When we stand on our toes the ball of our foot acts as the fulcrum. The effort needed to counteract the weight of the body is supplied by the calf muscle. The MA for this class of levers is greater than 1.

■ **Class 3** The effort is between the fulcrum and the load (*figure 1.5c*). The forearm, when the biceps is shortening, acts as a class 3 lever. The MA for this class of levers is less than 1.

In order to make calculations involving levers, we need to define the turning effect, or **moment**, of a force about any point:

moment = force × perpendicular distance

The **perpendicular distance** is measured between the line of action of the force and the point in question. Usually this point is described as the fulcrum (or pivot) only when it is actually the site of a hinge or joint.

The **principle of moments** states that in equilibrium the total clockwise moment about any point equals the total anticlockwise moment about that point.

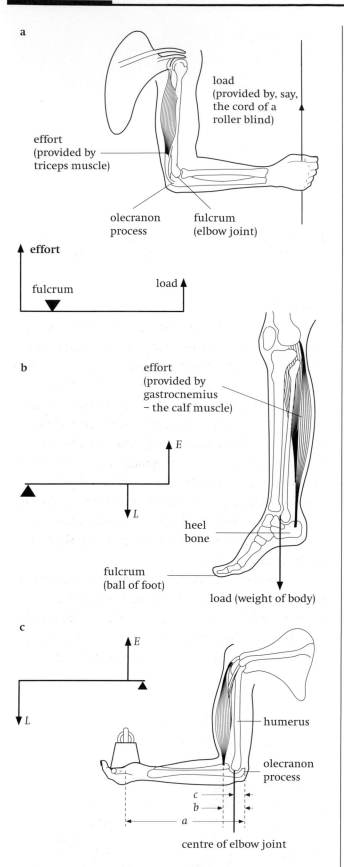

a effort (provided by triceps muscle)

olecranon process

fulcrum (elbow joint)

load (provided by, say, the cord of a roller blind)

effort

fulcrum

load

b effort (provided by gastrocnemius – the calf muscle)

E

L

heel bone

fulcrum (ball of foot)

load (weight of body)

c

E

L

humerus

olecranon process

c

b

a

centre of elbow joint

● **Figure 1.5** Levers. **a** Class 1 lever, load and effort on opposite sides of the fulcrum; **b** class 2 lever, load and effort on same side of the fulcrum, effort further than load, MA > 1; **c** class 3 lever, load and effort on same side of the fulcrum, effort nearer than load, MA < 1.

Worked example

Consider a mass of 5 kg held with forearm at right angles to the upper arm. It is possible using the principle of moments to calculate the muscular force of contraction M exerted by the biceps (*figure 1.6*). The following data are needed: the distance of M from the fulcrum F is 4 cm; the load W is exerted at a distance of 35 cm from F; the forearm has a mass of 1.5 kg, weight w, and a centre of mass that is 15 cm from the fulcrum. The acceleration due to gravity, g, is $9.8\,\mathrm{m\,s^{-2}}$ (or $\mathrm{N\,kg^{-1}}$).

Taking moments about F gives us
$$M \times 4 = 5 \times 9.8 \times 35 + 1.5 \times 9.8 \times 15$$
$$M = 484\,\mathrm{N}$$

This is approximately ten times the load. The reason is that the biceps exerts its force on the forearm at a point close to the elbow. This makes it much less effective in producing a rotation than forces exerted further from the elbow, such as the weight of the forearm and the load. To compensate, the biceps must exert a much larger force than would be necessary if it were attached further from the elbow.

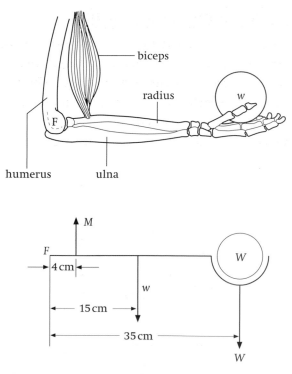

biceps

radius

w

F

humerus

ulna

M

F

4 cm

15 cm

35 cm

w

W

W

● **Figure 1.6** For the worked example, above.

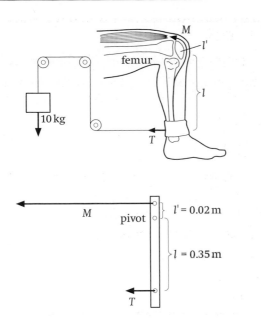

• **Figure 1.7** For *SAQ 1.2*. The muscular force *M* acts over the kneecap at a perpendicular distance *l'* from the pivot.

SAQ 1.2
An exercise device is used to strengthen the leg muscles (*figure 1.7*). Calculate the force *M* exerted by the muscle in the upper leg when moving the foot forward to lift the weight shown.

Standing, bending and lifting
The mechanics of the spine can be investigated by treating the spine approximately as a rigid rod. We can then apply Newton's first law (a body in equilibrium experiences no net force) and/or the principle of moments and deduce the forces involved in standing, bending and lifting.

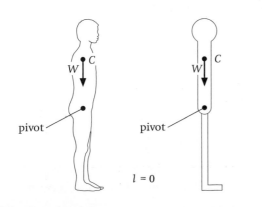

• **Figure 1.8** Standing.

• **Figure 1.9** In pregnancy the spine has to be tilted back to keep the centre of gravity over the middle of the foot.

Standing
When a person stands erect, as shown in *figure 1.8*, the weight of the upper body, *w*, is directly over the legs and little force is exerted by the back and leg muscles. Most of the body's weight is supported by the skeleton and not by muscle action. A vertical line from the centre of gravity of the upper body, *C*, passes through the middle of the foot. An overweight, or pregnant, condition leads to a forward shift in the centre of gravity *C*, moving the vertical projection of it forward to the ball of the foot, where the balance is less stable. To compensate the person may need to tip slightly backwards (*figure 1.9*).

The backbone or spine consists of 33 vertebrae of which nine are fused together to make the sacrum and the coccyx (*figure 1.10*). The sacrum is attached firmly to the pelvic girdle. The other 24 vertebrae are separate and are covered with

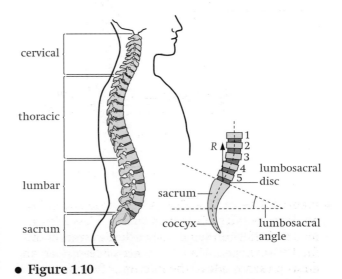

• **Figure 1.10**

cartilage; in between each are discs, tough fibrous pads. The discs allow some bending of the spine and cushion the bones from compression by the body's weight. The pressure on a disc in normal movement remains constant but if it increases to about 10^7 Pa then the disc will rupture.

When you are standing upright then the lumbrosacral disc, the disc next to the sacrum, lies at an angle to the horizontal of 40° (*figure 1.10*). The weight of the head, trunk and arms, about 0.6 times the total body weight T, acts via this disc on the sacrum and pelvis. Thus by Newton's third law, to every action there is an equal and opposite reaction, the reaction R of the pelvis and sacrum on the rest of the spine is also $0.6\,T$. This reaction can be resolved to give the forces parallel and perpendicular to the direction of the spine where it meets the pelvis (*figure 1.10*).

compressive force = $R \cos 40° = 0.46\,T$
shear force = $R \sin 40° = 0.39\,T$

If T is 700 N then R = 420 N and its components are a compressive force of 322 N and a shear force, across the lumbrosacral disc, of 270 N.

Bending and lifting

A range of muscles links the vertebrae of the spine to the pelvis. The spine can be considered as a more or less rigid structure pivoting at the lumbrosacral joint (*figure 1.11*). As mentioned above, the sacrum is attached firmly to the pelvic girdle and the top part of the pelvic girdle is attached to the muscles involved in bending and lifting.

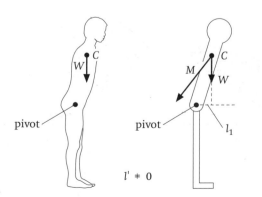

● **Figure 1.11** Bending. The pivot is the lumbroscral joint. The perpendicular distance of the upper body weight W from the fulcrum is l'.

The weight of the head, trunk and arms, which, as mentioned above, is 0.6 of the total body weight, acts at the centre of gravity of the upper body C. This point is about two-thirds the length t of the trunk from the buttocks. To a reasonable approximation, the resultant M of the forces exerted by the spinal muscles also acts at C and at an angle of 10° to the spine.

Suppose that the body is bent at an angle of 60° to the vertical (*figure 1.12a*). If a typical body mass of 70 kg is taken then the upper body weight W is $0.6 \times 70 \times 9.8 = 412$ N. The muscular force M can be found by balancing the moments of the forces about the pivot:

$$M \times 0.67t \sin 10° = W \times 0.67t \sin 60°$$

Thus

$$M = \frac{412 \sin 60°}{\sin 10°} = 2055 \text{ N}$$

Resolving forces parallel to the spinal column we obtain for the reaction force S of the pelvis on the spine (*figure 1.12b*)

$$S = M \cos 10° + W \cos 60° = 2230 \text{ N}$$

This large force causes the lumbrosacral disc to compress. As the angle of bending increases then the muscular effort and the reaction force on the lumbrosacral disc will increase. Clearly, the techniques involved in bending and lifting are important. If the legs are bent and the spine is kept almost vertical then the forces on the lumbrosacral disc and the other discs of the spine are reduced.

SAQ 1.3
A person has a mass of 75 kg for the trunk, head and arms. Calculate the muscular force M and the reaction force S on the lumbrosacral disc when the person bends to an angle of 70° to the vertical.

It is easy to adapt our calculations to describe the situation when a heavy object such as luggage is lifted. This is shown in *figure 1.12c*. Suppose that we now have a load L of, say, 196 N and the angle is still 60°. The forces acting on the spine are the upper body weight W plus load L, the muscular force M and the reaction force S on the lumbrosacral disc. Moments are again taken about the fulcrum:

$$M \times 0.67t \sin 10° = (412 + 196) \times 0.67t \sin 60°$$

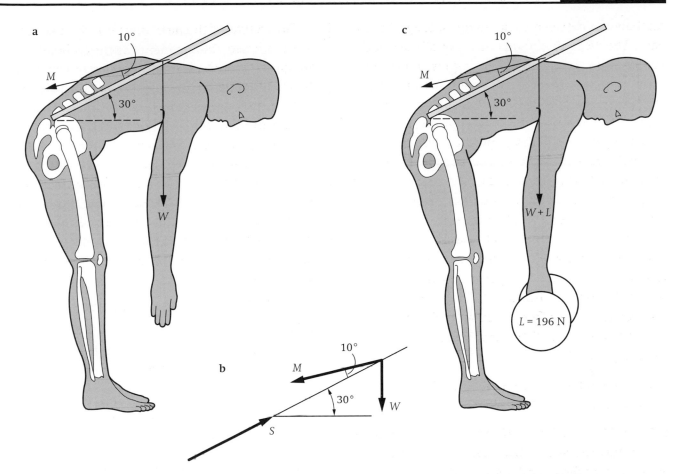

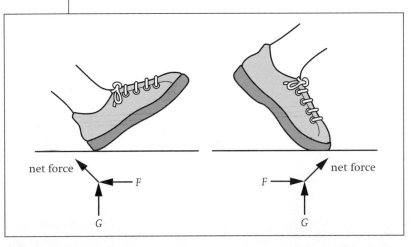

● **Figure 1.12** **a** Bending at an angle of 60° to the vertical; W is the upper body weight and M is the muscular force exerted on the spine, of length t. **b** Force diagram for the spine; S is the reaction force of the pelvis on the spine. **c** Lifting a load L. The forces W, M and L all act at roughly the same point.

This gives M as 3032 N. By resolving the forces parallel to the spine, it is then possible to calculate the new value of the reaction force S on the lumbrosacral disc:

$$S = M \cos 10° + (L + W) \cos 60°$$
$$= 3290 \, N$$

This force is eight times the upper body weight. Taking the cross-sectional area of the base of the spine to be $5 \, cm^2$, this gives a pressure of $7 \times 10^7 \, Pa$, according to our simplified model and would create problems for one or another disc if sustained for any length of time. The likely result would be a ruptured disc.

Walking and running

When standing the body weight is balanced by the **normal reaction** force of the ground. In equilibrium, this is equal and opposite to the body weight: it acts vertically upwards. When you start to move relative to the ground this force will change. When you leave the ground an upwards accelerating force is needed and when you land on the ground there will be a decelerating force (*figure 1.13*). Thus the normal

● **Figure 1.13** In walking, when the foot strikes the ground, friction acts backwards; when it leaves the ground, friction acts forwards.

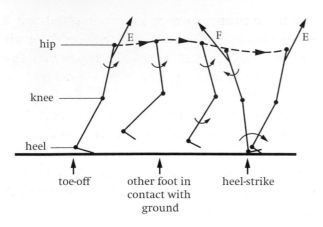

● **Figure 1.14** Action of the leg muscles in walking.

reaction is greatest just before the toe leaves the ground and when the heel strikes the ground.

The frictional force F is related to the normal reaction G by $F = \mu G$, where μ is the coefficient of static friction and has a value between 0.6 and 0.75 depending on the nature of the surface. Because F is proportional to G, it is a maximum when G is a maximum.

The resultant of F and G can be calculated using the rule for adding vectors; it will increase as you increase speed. If, however, there is a slippery surface then μ will be smaller. To avoid slipping, you need to walk with shorter strides because this requires less forward force than larger strides.

Steady walking

If you are walking at a steady speed then the force E of the hip muscle at the front of the leg swings the whole leg forward (*figure 1.14*). When this happens the leg rotates about the hip joint, with little force required. The lower leg is carried forward,

rotating about the knee, by the muscles of the upper leg and the ligaments of the knee joint. The upper leg then decelerates slowly by the action F of the hip muscles, and the lower leg by the action of the muscles around the knee. As the upper leg is pulled back the heel strikes the ground. When your foot strikes the ground it rolls from heel to sole to toe in contact with the ground; the whole action is then repeated.

When we walk we all have a natural period of oscillation that depends on the mass and length of our legs. Thus to avoid tiredness it is better to shorten one's stride rather than try to lengthen the time for each pace.

Running

However, to change from walking to running we do normally increase the number of strides we take per second. Typical speeds are:

walking, $1.5 \, \text{m s}^{-1}$
running, $6 \, \text{m s}^{-1}$
short sprint, $10 \, \text{m s}^{-1}$

To increase the length of stride, we leap forward and leave the ground for a short period of time. The inertia of the body mass keeps us moving forward. The centre of gravity C rises and falls on a slight curve. Generally the angle between the direction of leaping and the ground (the angle of projection) is kept fairly low since forward momentum is lost whenever a foot hits the ground. During the time that we are in the air one leg must move beneath us.

As in walking there is a rotation of the legs about the hip and knee joints (*figure 1.15*). At toe-off, the

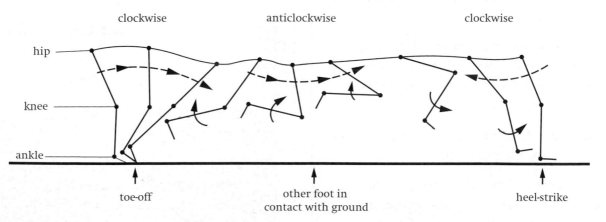

● **Figure 1.15** Action of the leg muscles in running. The labels 'clockwise' and 'anticlockwise' refer to the motion of the upper leg about the hip joint.

upper leg is moving clockwise, as viewed in the figure, about the hip joint. The upper leg then swings forwards anticlockwise, while the lower leg swings clockwise about the knee joint. At the extreme point (the third position from the right in the figure) the upper leg starts falling back clockwise again and the lower leg anticlockwise; the effect of the two opposite rotations brings the upper and lower leg into a nearly straight line for heel-strike. The leg now rotates clockwise about the point of contact with the ground until toe-off is reached again.

SUMMARY

◆ The basic mechanical structure of the human body consists of bones, ligaments, tendons, muscles and joints.

◆ Joints occur where the bones come together. Where a joint allows movement the bones are held by ligaments.

◆ Muscles are attached to bones by tendons. Muscles act in antagonistic pairs: one bends or flexes the joint, the other straightens the joint.

◆ The principle of moments and the concept of mechanical advantage can be applied to bones acting as levers.

◆ The forces on the spine involved in standing, bending and lifting can be calculated from Newton's first law (the net force on a body in equilibrium is zero) and the principle of moments.

◆ Correct body posture, particularly when lifting, requires the spine to be nearly vertical to avoid excess pressure on the discs of the spine.

◆ When standing the body weight is balanced by the normal reaction of the ground.

◆ In walking and running there are three external forces on the body: weight, normal reaction G and friction F. The latter two are related by $F = \mu G$.

When a runner reaches a constant speed only a small amount of energy is used in overcoming air resistance and producing the leap (*figure 1.15*). The main part of the energy expended is used in moving the legs.

The runner appears to rotate about a vertical axis if viewed from above. Moving the left arm forwards and the right arm backwards causes a clockwise rotation of the upper body. Reacting to this, the lower body rotates slightly in an anticlockwise direction and the right leg swings forward.

Questions

1 When you raise your arm there are three forces involved, as shown in *figure 1.16*. These are

W, the weight of the arm acting downwards

M, the force of the muscle acting at 15°

R, the force exerted by the shoulder on the humerus

The weight of the arm is 13 N. By resolving the force M of the muscle along the x and y axes, calculate M and R.

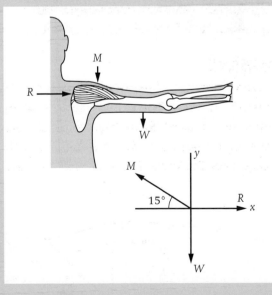

● **Figure 1.16**

2 Many injuries to the human body occur as a result of the incorrect lifting of heavy objects. Explain why the spine should be kept as vertical as possible during lifting to prevent such injuries.

CHAPTER 2

The eye

By the end of this chapter you should be able to:

1 understand and use the terms *principal focus*, *principal axis*, *optical centre* and *focal length* as applied to converging (convex) and diverging (concave) lenses;

2 recall and use the sign convention 'real is positive, virtual is negative';

3 recall and use the lens formula $\dfrac{1}{u} + \dfrac{1}{v} = \dfrac{1}{f}$;

4 recall the structure of the eye in terms of the *cornea*, *aqueous humour*, *iris*, *lens*, *ciliary muscles*, *vitreous humour*, *retina* and *optic nerve* and outline the function of each of these parts;

5 explain how the eye forms a focussed image of an object and how the eye adjusts for different distances;

6 understand and use the terms *near point*, *far point*, *depth of field* and *accommodation*;

7 distinguish between *short sight*, *long sight*, *presbyopia* and *astigmatism*;

8 describe and explain how these eye defects can be corrected by suitable lenses;

9 use the lens formula to calculate the focal length of the correcting lenses needed for long sight, short sight and presbyopia;

10 recall and use the equation relating the focal length of a lens to its power in dioptres, $P = 1/f$;

11 recall that the retina contains *rods* and three types of *cone*;

12 appreciate the role of the cones in the perception and differentiation of colour;

13 sketch and interpret a graph of the variation with wavelength of the relative responses of cones;

14 explain *scotopic* vision and *photopic* vision in terms of the action of rods and cones;

15 describe the response of rods and cones to variations in light intensity;

16 understand colour mixing by addition and by subtraction;

17 understand that the perception of colour and of light intensity has social implications, for example in advertising and in architecture.

The human eye

Our eyes have several features that are remarkable even when compared with the most advanced cameras.

- We can observe events over a very wide angle while seeing the detail of an object straight ahead.
- We have a rapid automatic focussing system and a built-in lens cleaner (blinking).
- Our eyes can operate over a large range of light intensities, from bright daylight to a very dark night (a ratio of 10^7 to 1).
- The cornea (see later) has a built-in scratch remover in that it is made of living cells and can repair any local damage.
- There is a self-regulating pressure system that maintains the pressure inside each eye.
- The brain uses the images from both eyes to give us three-dimensional perception.

The basic structure of the human eye is shown in *figure 2.1*. The key points are as follows.

- Light enters the eye at the **cornea**, where most of the **refraction** or bending of the light takes place. Refraction is discussed in *Physics 1*, chapter 18. The refractive index of the cornea is 1.37, which is large compared with that of air (refractive index 1.00) and so the cornea gives a large amount of refraction. In addition, its small radius of curvature increases the refractive

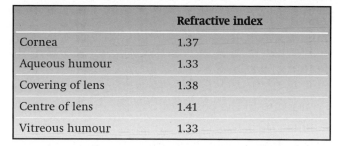

	Refractive index
Cornea	1.37
Aqueous humour	1.33
Covering of lens	1.38
Centre of lens	1.41
Vitreous humour	1.33

- **Table 2.1** Refractive indices of different parts of the eye.

effect. The refractive indices of the different parts of the eye are shown in *table 2.1*.

- The forward chamber of the eye is filled with **aqueous humour** and is divided into two parts by the **iris**. The aqueous humour is a clear, watery solution containing minute amounts of salts and has a refractive index of about 1.33. The iris controls the amount of light that enters the inner eye through the **pupil** (the hole in the centre of the iris). It is the coloured part of the eye.
- The **lens** is enclosed in a capsule and is attached by the **suspensory ligaments** to the circular **ciliary muscle**, which vary the thickness of the lens. Only a small amount of refraction takes place here. The lens can be regarded as a 'fine tuner'. In a normal eye, to focus a distant object the ciliary muscle relaxes, thus assuming its largest diameter. This pulls the suspensory ligaments outwards. These, in turn, pull on the edges of the lens, making it thinner (and of larger diameter). If, however, the object is close to the eye then the ciliary muscle contracts, the suspensory ligaments exert less tension on the lens and, by its natural elasticity, the lens becomes thicker and of smaller diameter. It thus has greater curvature and refracts light more. These changes in shape allow the eye to focus on both distant and near objects.
  - The light then passes through the posterior chamber, which is filled with a jelly-like substance called **vitreous humour** that maintains the spheroidal shape of the eye. Its refractive index is

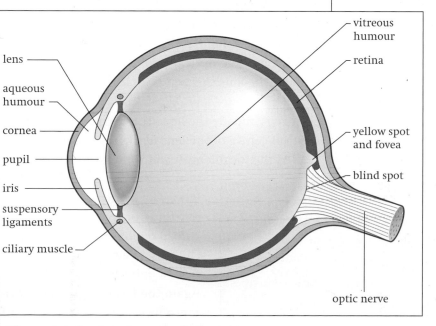

lens
aqueous humour
cornea
pupil
iris
suspensory ligaments
ciliary muscle

vitreous humour
retina
yellow spot and fovea
blind spot
optic nerve

- **Figure 2.1** Section through the human eye.

slightly greater than that of the aqueous humour (the difference occurs in the third decimal place) but both are approximately equal to that of water.

In the medical condition called glaucoma, the pressure in the posterior chamber increases; this alters the shape of the eye and interferes with the blood supply to the inner tissues of the eye.

■ Two types of special light-sensitive cell in the **retina** act as receptors for the optic nerve. These are called **cones** and **rods** and change the light into electrical impulses. Around the periphery of the retina, the receptors are mainly rods, which are sensitive to differing amounts of light. Moving inwards towards the optical axis there is an increasing proportion of the cells called cones. The cones are sensitive to the three colours red, green and blue. The other colours that we see are made up of different amounts of each of these colours. The signals from the cones enable the brain to interpret the colour of any object.

There are over 10^8 of these receptor cells in the retina, with rods outnumbering cones by about 20:1. A comparison of the properties of rods and cones is shown in *table 2.2*.

■ The **yellow spot** is an area of the retina about 1 mm in diameter and situated on the optical axis. At its centre is a tiny pit called the **fovea**. This is where we can see objects most clearly, as there is a high concentration of cone cells. In the middle of the fovea, an area called the foveola, each cone is connected to a separate nerve fibre whereas elsewhere in the retina many cones are connected to each nerve fibre. The density of cones in the foveola is about $150\,000\,\text{mm}^{-2}$. There are no rods present.

■ All the nerve fibres are gathered together into a bundle known as the **optic nerve**, which transmits the signals to the brain. The **blind spot** is where the optic nerve leaves the retina. There are no light-sensitive cells at the blind spot. The retinal artery and vein also pass through this point.

SAQ 2.1

a Explain clearly the difference between the cornea and the lens of the eye in terms of their ability to refract light.

b When you dive into water without a face mask objects are difficult to focus. With a face mask it is much easier. Explain why this is so, using the following information: the refractive index of water is 1.33, that of the cornea is 1.37 and that of air is 1.00.

Lenses

When light passes through a convex lens, the rays are refracted. This phenomenon is governed by the curvature of the lens and by its refractive index. One way to indicate the amount of refraction is to measure the focal length of the lens. A convex or converging lens makes light rays come together when they pass through the lens. The point where the rays meet is called the **focus**. When the rays come from a distant point, so far away that the rays are almost parallel, the focus is called the **principal focus**.

Rays that pass through the lens with only sideways displacement and no change in direction all go through the **optical centre** of the lens. For a symmetric lens this will be at its physical centre. For a 'meniscus' lens (*figures 2.6c, 2.7c*) the optical centre is outside the lens. The distance from the optical centre of the lens to the principal focus is called the **focal length** and is measured in metres (*figure 2.2a*). The central ray travels along the **principal axis**. For a diverging or concave lens the rays spread out after passing through the lens. They appear to diverge from a point behind the lens. Again the focal length is the distance from this point to the optical centre of the lens (*figure 2.2b*).

	Rods	Cones
Respond to	dim light	bright light
Maximum sensitivity	blue–green (500 nm)	green–yellow (560 nm)
Spatial resolution	low	good
Colour vision	none	needs at least two cone types
Rate of dark adaptation	about 15 minutes	about 5 minutes

● **Table 2.2** Properties of rods and cones.

a

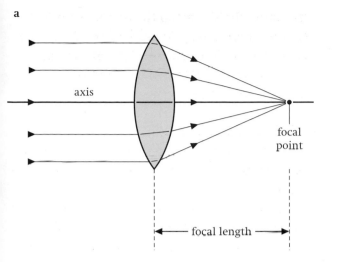

b

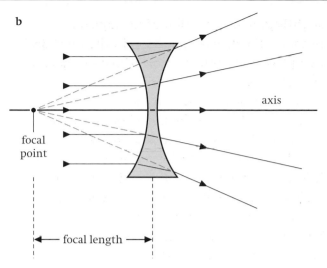

● **Figure 2.2** Focal length of **a** converging and **b** diverging lenses.

Focal length and power of a lens

In the 'average' eye, the focal length of the cornea is 2.2 cm and that of the eye lens is 5.5 cm. The combination of the two lenses has a focal length of 1.6 cm, because when lenses are combined their focal lengths add reciprocally (i.e the focal length f of the combination is given by $1/f = 1/f_1 + 1/f_2$). Thus it is convenient to use as a measure the **power** of a lens, where

$$\text{power} = \frac{1}{\text{focal length in metres}}$$

Power is measured in dioptres, symbol D. For a combination of lenses the powers can be added directly.

As the curvature of a lens increases, the focal length decreases and the power increases. A convex lens causes light to converge and its focal length and power are taken as positive. Because a concave lens causes light to diverge, its focal length and power must then be taken as negative.

Worked example

An optician places a convex lens of focal length 20 cm in front of a patient's eye. Calculate the power of this lens.

Focal length = 20 cm = 0.20 m, so

$$\text{power} = \frac{1}{\text{focal length in metres}}$$

$$= \frac{1}{0.20} = +5.0\,\text{D}$$

SAQ 2.2

A diverging lens has a power of −0.25 D. Calculate the focal length of this lens.

Depth of field

The most detail is seen when we focus straight ahead on a particular object, because then the light falls on the fovea. However, objects slightly further away and closer than the one we wish to see are also in focus. The distance over which an object can be moved and still be in focus is called the **depth of field** (*figure 2.3*). It is much greater for distant objects since then the extreme rays (the rays passing through the edges of the lens) from different objects enter at angles that are very similar and so the images are formed very close to each other, within the **depth of focus** of the retina. Close to the eye the angles of the extreme rays are very different, giving a very small depth of field. However, if a brighter light is used, so that the diameter of the iris aperture decreases, the depth of field increases (*figure 2.4*).

Accommodation

The ability of a lens to change its focal length is called accommodation. This general term also has an exact technical meaning, as we shall see below. The lens of the eye is made up of layers of transparent fibrous material, which can be compared to an onion. The average refractive index of the

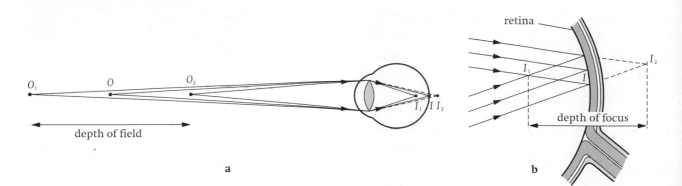

a

b

● **Figure 2.3** **a** Rays from O_1, O and O_2, far from the eye, are focussed at points I_1, I and I_2. O_1O_2 is the depth of field and I_1I_2 is the depth of focus. **b** The bundle of rays forms a circular **image patch** on the retina.

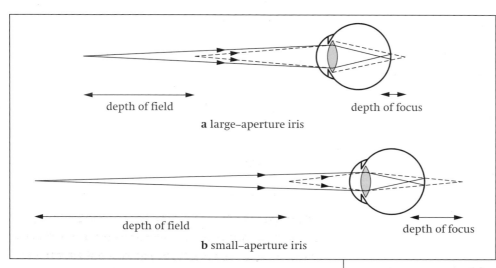

a large–aperture iris

b small–aperture iris

● **Figure 2.4** A smaller aperture of iris improves the depth of field, because the extreme rays are at smaller angles and because the depth of focus increases.

eye's lens is 1.413, but it varies slightly from edge to centre. The front surface of the lens is almost spherical. The rear surface is not so regular since it bulges near the centre.

The power of the lens varies with the tension in the surrounding ring of ciliary muscle, from about +20 to +30 dioptres. This change in power is called the **accommodation** of the eye and decreases with age.

When the ciliary muscle is relaxed and the lens is flattest and least powerful then the eye is said to be **unaccommodated** (*figure 2.5*). When the ciliary muscle is contracted, the eye has a greater power and is said to be **accommodated**. Notice that the process of accommodation for near objects is an active one and so leads to fatigue, whereas the unaccommodated eye can rest on remote objects without fatigue.

If the power of the cornea is added to that of the lens then the total power of the eye varies from about +60 D (unaccommodated) to +70 D (accommodated), giving an accommodation of 10 D. Accommodation by the eye can be contrasted

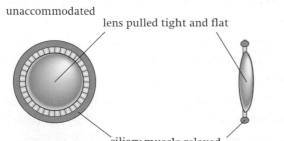

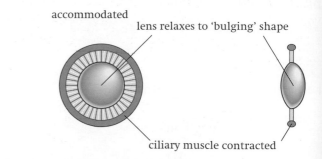

● **Figure 2.5** Changes in lens shape in the unaccommodated and accommodated eye. In the accommodated eye, the ring of ciliary muscle has a slightly smaller diameter (not shown).

with the action of a camera, where the power of the lens is fixed and the focussing is achieved by moving the lens towards or away from the film. A zoom lens has variable power in order to give variable magnification, but this is achieved by changing the distances between the lenses, not by changing the shape of the lens in a fixed position.

The lens formula

In solving problems for this and other situations, the thin-lens formula

$$\frac{1}{u} + \frac{1}{v} = \frac{1}{f}$$

is used, where

u is the distance from the lens to the object,
v is the distance from the lens to the image,
f is the focal length of the lens.

These quantities are illustrated as follows:

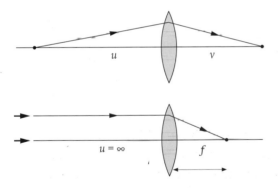

The 'real is positive' sign convention is used: real object and image distances and focal lengths are given a positive sign and virtual ones a negative sign.

We will now imagine that all the eye's refraction is due to a single thin lens; in fact this simple model gives reasonably good results. We first apply the lens formula to the unaccommodated eye, when the eye has its minimum power (about 60 D). Taking $u = \infty$, we can find the lens–retina distance v:

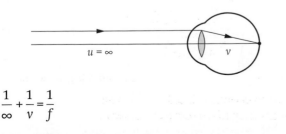

$$\frac{1}{\infty} + \frac{1}{v} = \frac{1}{f}$$

Since $1/\infty = 0$ and $1/f = 60\,D$,

$$v = \frac{1}{60} = 0.017\,m$$

This is often taken as 20 mm to simplify calculations.

Using the lens–retina distance, we can calculate the position u of the **near point**. This is the nearest distance at which we can focus the eye; in other words the eye is at maximum accommodation, with a power of about 70 D. Then

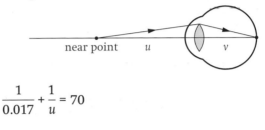

$$\frac{1}{0.017} + \frac{1}{u} = 70$$

Thus

$$60 + \frac{1}{u} = 70$$

$$\frac{1}{u} = 10$$

$$u = 0.10\,m$$

Although we can focus clearly on an object only 10 cm from our eyes, our eye muscles quickly tire at this degree of contraction. The nearest we can read in comfort for a long time is usually about 25 cm.

If you try to focus on a nearer object using both eyes then you will feel a strain caused by using the lateral muscles that make your two eyes converge. This is more tiring than the effect on the ciliary muscles, so in fact you automatically tend to close one eye.

Persistent eye strain that produces headaches can sometimes be due to weak muscles rather than refraction problems and can be helped by simple exercises like focussing both eyes on a pen as it is brought close to the nose or simply looking at the end of the nose.

There are no blood vessels in the lens so all the nutrients that reach the lens must diffuse in from surrounding tissue. As we become older, some cells in the centre of the lens become poorly nourished, die and turn white. Eventually the lens may become opaque; a cataract has formed. A plastic lens can be fitted inside the eye in place of the lens, which is removed.

The shape of the lens varies with age. In infancy, it is almost spherical, in adulthood it is of medium convexity and in old age it is considerably flattened. Young people have a much greater power of accommodation than adults and can read books held very close to their eyes. In middle age the lens becomes less flexible, so that accommodation decreases: the near point recedes until, usually, corrective lenses are required. This is discussed below.

SAQ 2.3

a Explain what is meant by *depth of field*, illustrating your answer with a diagram.

b Accommodation is the ability of the eye to change its focal length. How does the eye do this and why does the ability to accommodate change with age?

Eye defects and their correction

Short sight (myopia)

When a person can see near objects clearly but distant objects appear blurred they are said to be **short sighted**. Either the distance from the lens to the retina is too long or the cornea or lens is too convex and so the unaccommodated image is formed in front of the retina (*figure 2.6a*). To correct for this the power of the lens must be reduced and this requires that we add a diverging or concave lens to bring points at infinity to a focus further from the lens and so on to the retina (*figure 2.6b*).

Worked example

Suppose that a person's **far point**, which is the greatest distance at which the eye can focus, is at 0.2 m. The power of accommodation is 4 D. Calculate the power of the lens that is required to see distant objects clearly.

We use the lens formula, taking the image distance v in the eye, from lens to retina, as approximately 0.02 m. The focal length f_1 of the eye when unaccommodated can be found by putting $u = 0.2$ m and $v = 0.02$ m in the lens formula. This gives

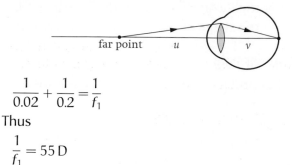

$$\frac{1}{0.02} + \frac{1}{0.2} = \frac{1}{f_1}$$

Thus

$$\frac{1}{f_1} = 55 \text{ D}$$

We want the far point to be at infinity, so the net power $1/f_2$ of the eye and the correcting lens must be given by the lens formula with $u = \infty$ and $v = 0.02$ m:

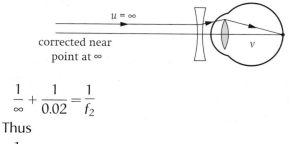

$$\frac{1}{\infty} + \frac{1}{0.02} = \frac{1}{f_2}$$

Thus

$$\frac{1}{f_2} = 50 \text{ D}$$

and so the person will need a lens of power -5 D, to give them a net power of 50 D when their eye is unaccommodated; they can then see distant objects clearly.

Thus, a diverging lens of the correct power causes distant rays to converge on the retina.

SAQ 2.4

A myopic person has a far point of 1.0 m. Taking the lens–retina distance as 2 cm, calculate the power of the lens needed to correct this eye defect.

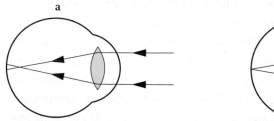

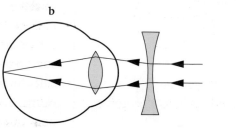

● **Figure 2.6 a** Short sight and **b** its correction with a concave lens. In practice, this lens is shaped as in **c**.

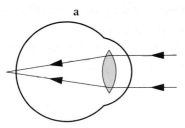 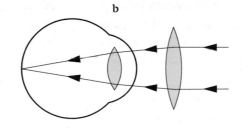

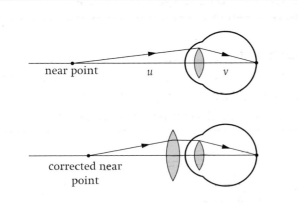

● **Figure 2.7 a** Long sight and **b** its correction with a convex lens. In practice the correcting lens is shaped as in **c**.

Long sight (hypermetropia)

When a person can see distant objects in focus but near objects appear blurred, they are said to have **long sight** (*figure 2.7a*). It is usually caused by a flattening of the lens or cornea or an eyeball which is too shallow.

As an object moves towards the eye, the eye must increase its power to keep the image on the retina. If the power of the cornea and lens is insufficient, as in hypermetropia, the image will appear blurred. The solution is to add a convex or converging lens of the correct power to focus the light on the retina (*figure 2.7b*).

Worked example

A person's **near point** – the shortest distance at which the eye can focus – is at 1.0 m from their eyes. For correct vision the near point should be 0.25 m from their eyes. Calculate the power of the correcting lens that is required.

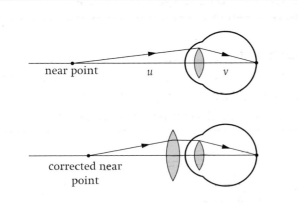

Here $u = 1.0$ m and $v = 0.02$ m; let f_1 be the focal length of the fully accommodated eye lens. Using the lens formula,

$$\frac{1}{1.0} + \frac{1}{0.02} = \frac{1}{f_1}$$

Thus

$$\frac{1}{f_1} = 51\,\text{D}$$

In order to focus on the retina objects at a distance of 0.25 m, the nett power of the eye lens and the correcting lens, $1/f_2$, must be given by the lens formula with $u = 0.25$ m and $v = 0.02$ m:

$$\frac{1}{0.25} + \frac{1}{0.02} = \frac{1}{f_2}$$

Thus

$$\frac{1}{f_2} = 54\,\text{D}$$

The difference in powers is +3 D and this is the power of the lens required to bring the near point from 1.0 m to 0.25 m.

SAQ 2.5

a A person who is long sighted has an accommodation of 3 D and a near point 2.0 m from their eyes. Calculate the power of the glasses needed to move the near point to 0.25 m from their eyes.

b Where is the far point when these glasses are worn?

Astigmatism

A person with astigmatism has difficulty in focussing light entering the eye in different planes. This happens because the cornea is distorted, so that the position of focus depends on the angle at which the light enters the eye (*figure 2.8*): if a vertical beam of light is focussed on the retina then a horizontal one will be focussed behind or in front of the retina. Light entering the eye from other angles will come to a focus between these two points.

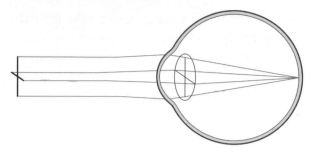

● **Figure 2.8** Astigmatism.

Astigmatism can be detected at an eyesight test by looking at a display of black lines radiating out like spokes from the centre of the field of view (*figure 2.9a*). If you suffer from astigmatism, you will perceive lines at some angles as darker and more distinct than those at other angles. This information can be used to determine the angle at which the axis of a **cylindrical** lens (*figure 2.9b*) must be positioned to correct the astigmatism.

SAQ 2.6

a A person who wears glasses removes them and holds them some distance from their eyes. They rotate the glasses while looking at an object through one lens. The object appears to change shape. Explain why this indicates that the person has astigmatism.

b Why is a lens which is not symmetrical used to correct this defect?

A typical prescription from an optician is shown in *table 2.3*.

The meaning of the terms in the prescription will now be explained for the right eye.

■ The negative 'sph' term indicates that the person is short sighted and needs a spherical lens with a power of −1.1 D to correct their distance vision.

■ The correction of +1.4 D means that the person requires a converging lens of this power to correct their near vision.

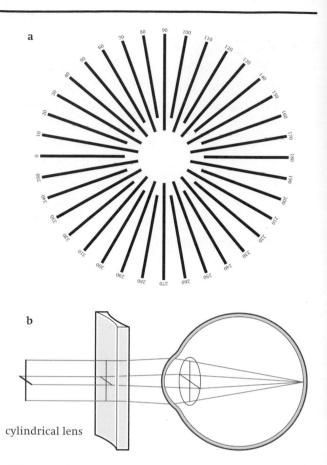

cylindrical lens

● **Figure 2.9 a** A simple test for astigmatism. An eye with astigmatism sees lines going in one direction more clearly than lines going in other directions. **b** Correction of astigmatism using a cylindrical lens.

■ The 'cyl' values are to correct the person's astigmatism and the 'axis' value indicates that the axis of the cylindrical correcting lens should be at 90° to the horizontal.

Similar terms apply to the left eye, and the 'prism' and 'base' values tell us that a **prism** component is needed in order for both eyes to see in the same direction.

The normal eye test simply determines what is called **visual acuity**, using a familiar chart of letters. Perfect vision is called 6/6 or 20/20. This means that at 6 m you can read the smallest size of type that a person with perfect vision can read (20/20 is the equivalent in feet). If your eyes test 6/12 then you can read at 6 m what a perfectly sighted person can read at 12 m.

Right eye					Left eye					
Sph	Cyl	Axis	Prism	Base		Sph	Cyl	Axis	Prism	Base
−1.1	−0.8	90			Distance	−1.1			1Δ	1 N
+1.4	−0.8	90			Near	+1.5				

● **Table 2.3** A typical prescription.

Presbyopia or 'old sight'

Although many people are hypermetropic from childhood, even more become long sighted as they grow older, and may be seen to be holding books further and further away until their arm is not long enough! Their eyes are gradually losing the power of accommodation, a condition known as **presbyopia**. Remember that in a fully accommodated eye the elasticity of the lens has allowed it to assume its most curved shape (*figure 2.5*).

In infants the lens is very elastic, the power of accommodation is great and the child can focus on objects very close to its eye. Telling children not to hold books too close to their eyes is unimportant since they are merely making full use of their youthful abilities.

We have an accommodation of about 14 D at age eight but this drops to 3 D when we are in our forties (*figure 2.10*). So, for reading, glasses that will increase the power of the accommodated eye are needed. However, many people who develop presbyopia already suffer from eye defects; for example, they may have myopia, so that now they can

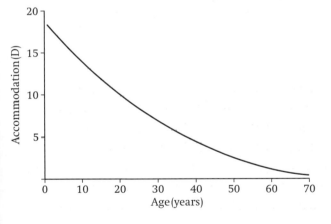

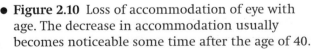

● **Figure 2.10** Loss of accommodation of eye with age. The decrease in accommodation usually becomes noticeable some time after the age of 40.

see clearly neither at a distance nor close up. For the myopia they need a negative-power lens and for the presbyopia a positive-power lens – contradicting requirements! However, distant objects are often in the centre of the field of vision, or above centre, while reading materials can be held below the centre. Therefore **bifocal** glasses can be used, in which the positive-power lens to correct for presbyopia is inserted as a segment at the lower part of the main lens. Correcting lenses can be made with more than two segments, or even a smooth gradation from positive to negative so that the distinctive line on the glasses is not visible; such lenses are called **varifocal**.

The various defects are summarised in *table 2.4*.

Contact lenses

The idea of lenses placed directly in contact with the eye is not new. In 1508 Leonardo da Vinci noticed that if he placed his face in a glass bowl of water and opened his eyes his vision improved. It was not until the 20th century, however, that the first contact lenses appeared. Initially they were made of glass and covered most of the eye but modern lenses are made of plastic and cover the iris only.

Contact lenses can be used to correct eyesight defects in a similar way to spectacle lenses. They are placed in front of the cornea and are much smaller and thinner than ordinary lenses, about 1 mm thick and 1 cm in diameter. They are held in place on the tear film (the layer of fluid) on the eye by surface tension forces and effectively become part of the cornea.

The reason that thinner lenses can be used is that the distance between the correcting lens and

Focussing problem	Common name	Cause	Correction required
Myopia	short sight	long eyeball or excess curvature of eyeball	concave lens
Hypermetropia	long sight	short eyeball or insufficient curvature of cornea	convex lens
Astigmatism	–	unequal curvature of cornea	cylindrical lens
Presbyopia	old age vision	lack of accommodation	bifocals

● **Table 2.4** Common eye defects and their corrections.

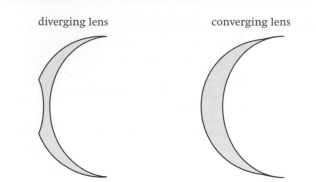

diverging lens   converging lens

● **Figure 2.11** Cross-section of contact lenses.

the cornea is smaller. To correct for myopia a weaker lens is now needed but for hypermetropia a stronger lens. The curvatures of the lens surfaces are different, the inner surface being made to fit the shape of the cornea (*figure 2.11*). Since the lens moves with the eye, the aberrations or faults that occur at the edges of a powerful spectacle lens are eliminated.

There are different types of contact lens. **Hard** contact lenses are made of a tough plastic. It can be difficult to get used to wearing them but they last a long time. Astigmatism is corrected since the light now enters the eye through a rigid spherical surface. **Gas-permeable** contact lenses are made of a material that is again rigid but allows more oxygen to flow to the cornea. **Soft** contact lenses are made of a special plastic that allows a lot of oxygen to pass through to the cornea, so that the lenses can be worn for a long period of time. Their shape can adjust somewhat to any small changes in the curvature of the cornea, so they are more comfortable. However, since the cornea may be irregular and these lenses do not maintain a spherical surface, they do not correct for astigmatism. Furthermore, they deteriorate more rapidly than hard contact lenses and suffer from protein build up, but the advent of disposable lenses means that this is no longer a problem.

The latest products can be tinted and can vary in external curvature like varifocal spectacle lenses.

Correction without surgery

Some people find that contact lenses cause irritation, and eye surgery can create problems. One solution is to use night-time contact lenses that can reshape the cornea. This new technique is called **orthokeratology** and uses reverse-geometry gas-permeable hard contact lenses to change the shape of the cornea. Only myopia can be corrected in this way. The contact lens is not a normal concave lens but shaped like a brimmed hat with a flat top above the cornea. There are two steep sides and a double rim that grips the cornea by surface tension. The pressure on the eyeball flattens the cornea. The contact lens must be worn every night or the cornea will revert back to its original shape. The technique can only be used for those with low or moderate myopia and is particularly useful for sports players or those in an occupation where contact lenses would prove difficult, such as firefighting. A significant advantage is that the change is not permanent: the contact lenses must be used continuously to retain the effect. If surgical techniques are used and problems arise then these problems are generally irreversible. Such techniques, which use lasers, are dealt with in chapter 10.

Colour perception

There is a complex relationship between our perception of colour and the perceived qualities of hue, brightness and saturation. **Hue** is what we call colour and is determined by the wavelength of the light. It includes the basic colours of the spectrum together with others, such as the shades of magenta formed by mixing violet and red from the opposite ends of the spectrum. **Brightness** is the subjective impression of light intensity (the power per unit area reaching the retina). **Saturation** is the purity of the colour. When mixed with a neutral colour, white, grey or black, the colour becomes less saturated.

The cornea is opaque to wavelengths shorter than 300 nm and the lens is opaque to wavelengths below 380 nm. The long-wavelength limit would be set by absorption of light by the water in the corneal fluid but in any case the light-sensitive cells in the retina do not respond to wavelengths above 760 nm. The highest sensitivity (maximum response) of the eye occurs at 550 nm, which corresponds to green-yellow light.

Colour perception is made possible by the existence of three different types of cone, which

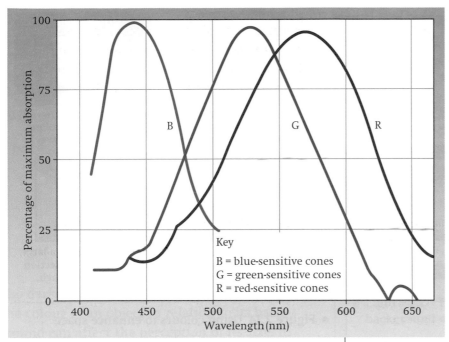

● **Figure 2.12** Ranges of sensitivity for the three different types of cone.

respond respectively to blue, green and red light. Each type of cone has its own photosensitive pigment:

blue-sensitive cones contain cyanolabe;
green-sensitive cones contain chlorolabe;
red-sensitive cones contain erythrolabe;

Each one absorbs light over a range of wavelengths; the peaks are at 445 nm, 535 nm, and 575 nm respectively. The absorption of light produces a chemical change in the pigment molecule, causing a small electrical potential to be developed, which is transmitted to the brain by the nerves. The pigment molecule is subsequently regenerated.

The sensitivity of the cones varies with wavelength, as shown in *figure 2.12*. It can be seen that light of, say, 500 nm wavelength will excite all three types of cone whereas light of 600 nm will excite only the red and green cones. The brain processes the relative strengths of the signals to determine the colour of the object.

When the three **primary** colours of light, red, green and blue, are added in equal proportions they give the sensation of white light. In pairs, we have

green + blue = cyan
blue + red = magenta

red + green = yellow.

Cyan, magenta and yellow are **secondary** colours obtained by the **addition** of wavelengths. Each secondary colour has a **complementary** primary; when the two are added in the correct proportions, white light is obtained. Thus

cyan + red = white
magenta + green = white
yellow + blue = white.

Any colour of light can be matched by a combination of the primaries red, green and blue. This is used in colour television and photography. In *figure 2.13* the three primaries define a triangle with white in the centre.

SAQ 2.7

a Why do the lenses of most sunglasses appear green?

b What is the chemical basis for colour vision?

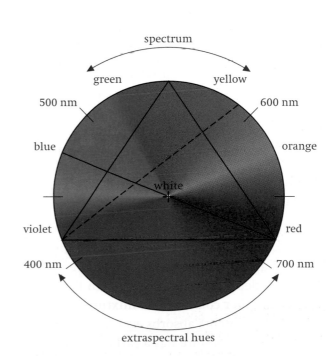

● **Figure 2.13** The colour triangle. The extraspectral hues shown are formed from combinations of wavelengths at the ends of the visible spectrum.

● **Figure 2.18** **a** and **b**: Colour has been used in different ways to create an unusual atmosphere in these two restaurants. **c** and **d**: Colour is used in advertising to attract different groups.

Perception of light intensity

Rods contain the photosensitive pigment **rhodopsin** (sometimes called **visual purple**). Rhodopsin is broken down when illuminated and this action starts a nerve impulse in the nerve cell attached to the rod. Nerve impulses from the rods travel along the optic nerve to the brain, which interprets the signals as a pattern of brightness or light intensity. Rods react over a wide range of wavelengths (*figure 2.19*) and respond to much lower levels of light intensity than the cones. So in dim light we can detect the shape of objects but not their colour. This is known as **scotopic vision**.

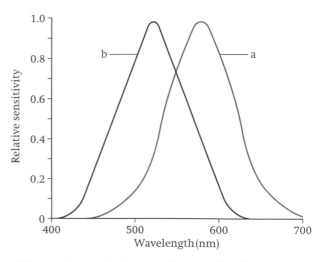

● **Figure 2.19** Relative sensitivity of **a** light-adapted and **b** dark-adapted eye.

The perception of light intensity is not related simply to the amount of light entering the eye. The reason is that the rods adapt to the prevailing light intensity. At high light levels the rhodopsin remains broken down, so that a rod cannot respond to further stimulation by light. In dim or dark conditions, however, the rhodopsin can reform and the rod is ready again to respond to stimulation by light. This means that rods are more sensitive at low light levels.

The cones respond at high light levels and the rods are then not so important in the reception of light. This is known as **photopic vision**. If the light level is very high, then damage to the eye will occur. The differences between scotopic and photopic vision are summarised in *table 2.5*.

The importance of the context in the perception of brightness can be demonstrated using *figure 2.20*. This shows three identical grey circles, which are viewed against backgrounds that reflect different amounts of light. Note that although all the grey circles reflect an equal amount of light, the brightness of each appears to be different because the brain interprets them in relation to their surroundings. This helps the brain to distinguish shape and movement at low light levels.

When the background source of light is very low then a large change in intensity of the source is needed in order to perceive that any change has occurred. In a very dark room there has to be a change of 1000% in the source intensity before we would notice it. In a brightly lit room, however, even a 1% change might be noticed.

Architecture

The brain also interprets the perceived light intensity in other ways. For example, brighter objects are perceived to be lighter in weight or nearer than darker objects of the same size. This effect

● **Figure 2.20** Effect of background on the perception of light intensity.

can be used to produce visual illusions in architecture, as shown in *figure 2.21*.

The impact of architectural features relies to an important extent on **visual edges**. Two types of visual edge are possible: **reflectance** edges, which arise from the different amounts of light *reflected* from two adjacent surfaces such as a white surface on a grey background; and **illumination** edges, which arise from different amounts of light *falling* on the surfaces such as occurs when shadows fall across the surface of a building.

Visual edges can emphasise patterns and can lead the eye in a certain direction; they can create dramatic and beautiful effects (*figure 2.21*).

SAQ 2.9
Cathedrals and churches are often designed to give an impression of space, beauty and restfulness. What features of architecture and colour help this effect?

● **Figure 2.21** Use of light and shadow in architecture.

Scotopic vision	Photopic vision
uses rods	uses cones mainly
night vision	daytime vision
distinguishes only light and shadow	distinguishes colours
little detail seen	large amount of detail seen

● **Table 2.5**

SUMMARY

◆ In the eye, the cornea does most of the refraction and the lens acts as a fine tuner for focussing, since it can change shape by use of the ciliary muscle. Rods and cones in the retina receive the light and send electrical impulses to the brain.

◆ Converging or convex lenses bring parallel rays of light to a point on the principal axis called the principal focus.

◆ Diverging or concave lenses make parallel rays diverge so that they appear to come from a point behind the lens, again called the principal focus.

◆ The distance from the optical centre of the lens to the principal focus is called the focal length.

◆ The power of a lens in dioptres

$$= \frac{1}{\text{focal length in metres}}$$

◆ The depth of field is the distance over which objects in front of and behind the object that is being viewed is in focus.

◆ Accommodation is the ability of the lens to change shape; it is defined as the maximum change in power of an eye lens.

◆ Short sight (myopia) occurs when near objects can be seen clearly but distant objects are blurred. Correction is by a concave (negative-power) lens.

◆ Long sight (hypermetropia) occurs when, in youthful vision, distant objects can be seen clearly but near objects are blurred. Correction is by a convex lens.

◆ Astigmatism occurs when the curvature of the cornea is unequal in perpendicular directions. Correction is by a cylindrical lens.

◆ In presbyopia, the near point recedes with age. Correction is by a convex lens.

◆ Correction of eye defects can be made using contact lenses.

◆ Colour is determined by wavelength and detected in the eye by three types of cone, sensitive to red, green and blue light; these are the three primary colours of light.

◆ The perception of colour has social implications. Bright colours create a perception of movement and busyness while pastel colours create space and calm. These effects are used in interior design and advertising.

◆ About 10% of males, but very few females, are affected by colour blindness.

◆ At low intensities, vision is scotopic; at high intensities it is photopic.

◆ The brain to some extent processes light-intensity data according to context.

◆ Visual edges are important in architecture.

Questions

1 a Describe the main features of the eye and in particular how the lens and cornea contribute to vision.

 b A man is long sighted. The closest distance at which he can focus is 150 cm; in normal vision this would be 25 cm. Calculate the power and focal length of the correcting lens needed.

2 The entrance hall in a hospital is to have three areas. One room is to be designed as a busy admissions area that can handle large numbers of patients quickly, but without causing stress. In a second room patients will wait for treatment. A third room is to be used as a small play area for children. Describe any features of colour and architecture that you should take into account in the design of each room.

The ear

By the end of this chapter you should be able to:

1 describe how the ear acts as a *transducer* to an incoming sound wave;

2 explain what is meant by *frequency response*;

3 appreciate the wide range of intensities that can be detected by the ear;

4 remember the orders of magnitude of the minimum detectable intensity of hearing I_0 (the *threshold intensity*) and of the intensity at which *discomfort* is experienced;

5 understand the significance of the *logarithmic response* of the ear to intensity;

6 use the equation

intensity level $= 10 \log_{10} (I/I_0)$

where I is the intensity level and I_0 is the threshold intensity level in *decibels* (dB);

7 understand that *loudness* is the subjective response of a person to frequency and to intensity level;

8 sketch and interpret a graph of the change in intensity level with frequency;

9 understand that frequency response and minimum detectable intensity are influenced by factors such as age and exposure to noise.

The ear as a transducer

Sound is a longitudinal pressure wave, which is propagated through a medium (usually air) by the oscillation of particles of the medium. Further properties of sound waves are detailed in chapter 19 of *Physics 1*. The function of the ear is to amplify the small pressure changes it receives and to change them into electrical signals that can be interpreted by the brain. Thus the ear acts as a **transducer**, converting one form of energy into another: the sound energy is converted into electrical energy.

Structure of the ear

The structure of the ear enables a large range of frequencies to be detected and permits the listener to locate a specific sound.

A section through a human ear is shown in *figure 3.1*. It can be divided into three parts.

- The **outer ear** collects and directs the sound to the middle ear.
- The **middle ear** amplifies the sound and provides **acoustic matching** between the outer and inner ear. Acoustic matching means that the sound waves are largely transmitted through the different parts of the ear with little reflection of energy.
- The **inner ear** is concerned with the conversion of sound energy into electrical energy and also with balance.

The sense of hearing involves:

- a mechanical system that stimulates hair cells in the inner ear;
- sensors that produce changes in the electrical potentials of the auditory nerves;
- the auditory cortex, which is the part of the brain that interprets and decodes the signals from the auditory nerve.

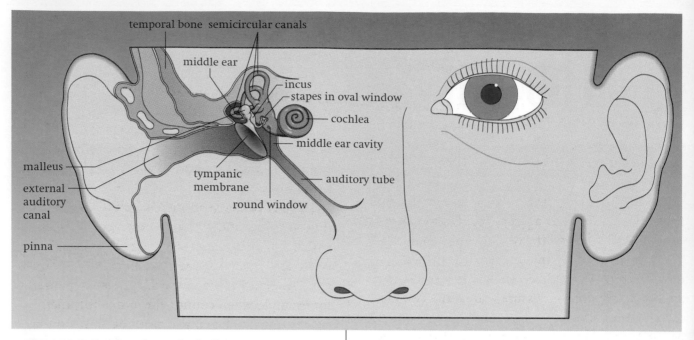

● **Figure 3.1** Section through the human ear.

Outer ear

The outer ear consists of the **pinna**, which is used to collect sounds and direct them down the **auditory canal** to a diaphragm called the **eardrum** or **tympanic membrane**. This is a thin flexible layer of fibrous tissue covered externally by skin and internally with mucous membrane. The outer ear acts like an ear trumpet or horn since the sound enters an opening of large cross-sectional area and goes along a tube of gradually decreasing cross-sectional area.

The gain, or relative increase in pressure, produced by the outer ear is quite large (approximately 20) at a frequency of 3 kHz. Towards the upper and lower ends of the speech-frequency spectrum the gain is much lower. A larger pinna would improve the gain for sounds coming from the forward direction. Cupping a hand behind the ear gives an effect somewhat similar to a larger pinna and is useful when the voice of a speaker seems to be just below the level of surrounding noise.

Resonance

The peak in the gain at 3 kHz is, in part, due to the **resonance** of the auditory canal. Although it is quite a complex shape and the closed end is not rigid but a thin diaphragm, there is a resemblance to an organ pipe closed at one end. Resonance occurs when source waves in a structure are amplified by virtue of the shape or construction of the structure. Resonance for a particular structure will only occur at a particular set of frequencies. It is explained in detail in chapter 20 of *Physics 1*.

The lowest resonant frequency is the **fundamental**, which in the case of the auditory canal is 3 kHz. Taking the length of the ear canal to be 2.5 cm, the fundamental resonance wavelength can be calculated since the first resonance position occurs when this length corresponds to a quarter wavelength. The fundamental wavelength would thus be 4 × 2.5 = 10 cm. Using the equation $f = v/\lambda$ then gives for the fundamental resonance frequency f about 3.3 kHz if the speed of sound is taken as 330 m s^{-1}.

Since the diaphragm is not rigid but flexible (otherwise we would not hear anything), and the tube is not of uniform diameter, the calculation can only be approximate. Nevertheless, the calculated resonant frequency is close to that found in practice.

SAQ 3.1

Describe the key features of the shape of the outer ear and state the functions of this part of the ear. Explain the use of the term *resonance* when applied to this part of the ear.

Middle ear

The middle ear (*figure 3.2*) is an irregularly shaped, air-filled bony cavity, called the **tympanic cavity**, which contains a set of three bones known as the **ossicles**. These bones are the **malleus** (hammer), the **incus** (anvil) and the **stapes** (stirrup). The middle ear acts as an acoustic matching device between the air-filled outer ear and the fluid-filled inner ear.

The bones act as a lever system, amplifying the force received on the eardrum by a factor of about 1.3 and applying it to the **oval window** (*figure 3.3*). The area of the tympanic membrane is about 65 mm^2 while that of the oval window is just over 3 mm^2. Since force = pressure × area, the two factors give a pressure increase of between 25 and 30, as needed to transmit the vibrations through the cochlear fluid in the inner ear.

The middle ear also contains two muscles that help to protect against excessively loud sounds, which can cause damage to the delicate hearing mechanism. One muscle tightens the eardrum and decreases the transmission of low-frequency sound to the bones. The other pulls on the stapes and reduces the sound intensity reaching the inner ear. This change is not instantaneous and takes about 50 milliseconds, so that the ear is protected against gradual sound changes, but not against rapid changes such as would result from explosions.

These same muscles also protect our ears from our voices. The vibrations in the vocal tract are transmitted through the head to the ears and would sound extremely loud, except that the muscles are automatically activated before the sounds start and so protect you against the sound of your own voice.

The middle ear is connected to the back of the mouth by the **auditory tube** (Eustachian tube), which equalises the pressure on each side of the eardrum. If the pressures are not equal, we experience discomfort. When the air pressure changes, for example when coming down in a lift, then swallowing (or chewing) causes the valve on the tube to open and the symptoms of the pressure change are relieved.

SAQ 3.2

When people are suffering from a cold they often experience discomfort in their ears in an aircraft. Explain why this occurs and what they could do to help reduce the pain.

Inner ear

The inner ear is a fluid-filled cavity within the skull (which affords protection) and contains the vestibule, the cochlea and the semicircular canals (*figure 3.3a*). The **vestibule** is a cavity lying between the oval window and the cochlea and connects with all the other chambers. The **semicircular canals** are the sensors for the balance-control mechanism and are three liquid-filled tubes set at right angles to each other. As you move your head the liquid moves; small hairs in the canals detect the changes and trigger nerve impulses, which are sent to the brain where they initiate the reflex actions that maintain balance. Two small sacs at the base of the semicircular canals register the position of the head relative to the upright position.

The **cochlea** is so called because it is shaped like a coche, a snail's shell. It is a fluid-filled **three-chambered** tube twisted into a spiral of approximately $2\frac{3}{4}$ turns; the diameter of the tube

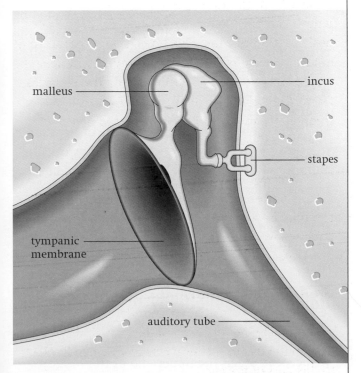

● **Figure 3.2** Section through the middle ear.

malleus

incus

stapes

tympanic membrane

auditory tube

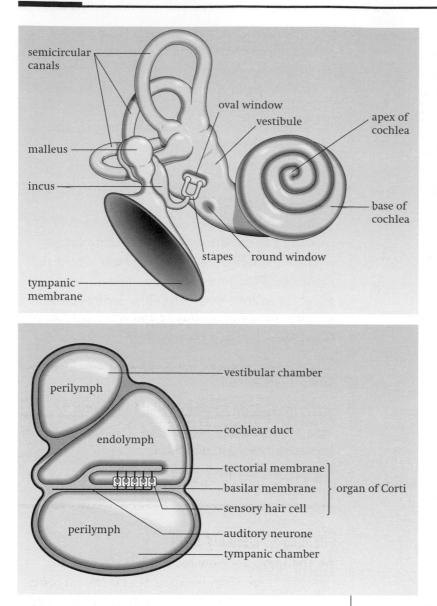

● **Figure 3.3 a** The inner ear; **b** section through the cochlea.

decreases from base to apex (*figure 3.3a*). Two of the chambers, the **vestibular** and **tympanic** chambers, are joined together at the apex of the spiral; the clear fluid filling both is called perilymph.

The base of the vestibular chamber connects with the oval window and the base of the tympanic chamber connects with the round window. Between these two chambers is the **cochlear** duct, filled with a fluid known as endolymph or **cochlear fluid**.

The **basilar membrane** (*figure 3.3b*) separates the cochlear duct from the tympanic chamber and is composed of vibration-sensitive cells. A single layer of sensory cells lies on the inner surface of the basilar membrane. These '**hair cells**' (so-called because they resemble very fine hairs) project across the endolymph-filled duct to the **tectorial membrane**,

which is the wall between the cochlear duct and the vestibular chamber. The **nerve fibres** at the base of the hair cells generate nerve impulses, which are fed to the brain via the auditory nerve. This structure is known as the **organ of Corti**.

As mentioned earlier, the increase in pressure achieved by the middle ear is necessary since the stapes has to produce vibrations – a longitudinal wave – in the cochlear fluid (remember that fluids have a greater inertia than air). The waves travel along the vestibular and tympanic chambers and excite the hair cells to send signals along the auditory nerve. Exactly how the cochlea works is not well understood but it is known that higher frequencies excite the cells nearest to the base of the cochlea and lower frequencies excite those nearest to the apex. A group of cells sends an impulse to the brain, which determines the frequencies present by locating the areas sending the sounds. An increase in loudness is detected in several ways:

■ firstly, there is an increase in the amplitude of the signal generated by each hair cell;
■ secondly, a greater proportion of the hair cells in the appropriate area are stimulated;
■ thirdly, hair cells in adjacent areas also are stimulated.

Since the cochlea lies within the bone of the skull, it is possible to excite the cochlear fluid by causing vibrations in the bone itself. This can be accomplished by, for example, placing a tuning fork against the part of the skull behind the ear called the mastoid. Sound will be heard at the frequency of the tuning fork.

Range and sensitivity of hearing

The normal frequency range of hearing is from about 20 Hz to 20 000 Hz (20 kHz) for adults. As we become older, the upper end of the range normally falls to about 15 kHz or below.

The human ear can distinguish a remarkably small change in frequency; this is termed the **frequency response** of the ear. It is about 0.1% at any given frequency. This can be compared with a musical semitone, which is a frequency change of about 6%; a tone is from doh to ray (the first two notes of a musical scale). From 60 to 1000 Hz we can distinguish differences of 2–3 Hz. Beyond 1000 Hz it is more difficult to distinguish between frequencies that are close together.

Sound intensity is a measure of the sound power crossing unit area. The minimum detectable intensity at a given frequency is called the threshold intensity of hearing. It is shown as a function of frequency in *figure 3.4*, plotted on a logarithmic scale. The reason for using this type of scale is that the range of frequencies heard is very large and would be difficult to plot on a linear scale. The graph shows that the human ear is most sensitive at about 2 kHz.

At low intensities, very small changes in the intensity will be detected but at high intensities the same change may not be noticed. The reason is that equal changes in intensity are not perceived as equal changes in loudness. The relationship between intensity and loudness is, as we shall see, approximately logarithmic, so ten times the intensity is perceived to be only about twice as loud.

Intensity level – the decibel

At about 1000 Hz the threshold intensity I_0 is $10^{-12}\,\mathrm{W\,m^{-2}}$. The **intensity level** in **bels** of a sound of intensity I is defined with reference to this threshold intensity, as follows:

$$\text{intensity level in bels} = \log_{10}\frac{I}{I_0}$$

Since the bel (B) is a large unit, the one normally used is the **decibel** (dB): 1 B = 10 dB. Then

$$\text{intensity level in decibels} = 10\log_{10}\frac{I}{I_0}$$

The bel is named after Alexander Graham Bell, who invented the telephone and was a teacher of the deaf.

Worked example

A sound has an intensity of $1.0 \times 10^{-7}\,\mathrm{W\,m^{-2}}$. Calculate the intensity level.

The intensity level in decibels is

$$10\log_{10}\frac{10^{-7}}{10^{-12}} = 10\log_{10}10^5 = 50\,\mathrm{dB}$$

Changes in intensity level

We shall now see how to calculate changes in intensity level. First, we show that if the intensity is doubled then the intensity level is increased by about 3 dB.

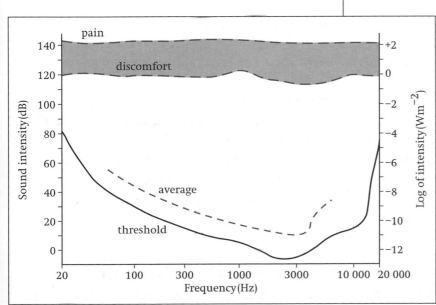

● **Figure 3.4** Sensitivity of the human ear. The solid curve shows the threshold intensity level for a young person with good hearing. The broken curve gives the average threshold for all people.

Worked example

Two television sets are showing different programmes; the sound intensity from each set is $I = 1.0 \times 10^{-7}\,W$. Calculate the total intensity level.

The intensity level of each set is the same as that calculated in the worked example above, 50 dB. When both sets are on, the total intensity will be $I + I = 2I$. Thus

total intensity level in dB $= 10\log_{10}(2I/I_0)$

$= 10\log_{10} 2 + 10\log_{10}(I/I_0)$

$= 10\log_{10} 2 +$ intensity level of either TV set by itself

$= 3 + 50$

$= 53\,dB$

We have the perhaps surprising result that *doubling* the intensity leads to only a 3 dB increase in the intensity level, which is closely related to the increase in loudness (see below).

Noise level (dB)	Situation
0	minimum sound that can be heard
10	movement of leaves in trees
20	a quiet lane
30	whispering
40	an ordinary conversation
50	noise in the average home
60	normal conversation at 1 m
70	inside a large shop
80	about 18 m from a busy motorway
85	the first danger level
90	inside a heavy truck or underground train
100	a lorry at a distance of 8 m in a narrow street
110	a pop group at 1 m or a train whistle at 15 m
120	an aircraft at 175 m
130	a jet engine at 35 m

● **Table 3.1** Typical noise levels for different situations. A sustained noise level above about 85 dB may cause permanent damage to the inner ear. At 100 to 110 dB conversation becomes impossible.

SAQ 3.3

When new windows were put into a house, the intensity of sounds measured in a room changed from $10^{-4}\,W\,m^{-2}$ to $10^{-7}\,W\,m^{-2}$. Calculate the change in intensity level in decibels by subtracting the old intensity level from the new intensity level.

As in *SAQ 3.3*, the difference in intensity level between two sounds, of intensities say I_1 and I_2, can be calculated by subtraction: we obtain

$$\text{change in intensity level} = 10\left(\log_{10}\frac{I_2}{I_0} - \log_{10}\frac{I_1}{I_0}\right)$$

On using $\log(a/b) = \log a - \log b$ this becomes

$$\text{change in intensity level} = 10\log_{10}\frac{I_2}{I_1}$$

Typical **noise intensity levels** are given in *table 3.1*.

The human ear can respond to intensities of sound ranging from as low as $10^{-12}\,W\,m^{-2}$ to as high as $1\,W\,m^{-2}$. Our hearing response is subjective but there are three thresholds (*figure 3.4*). As mentioned above the **threshold of hearing** is the minimum intensity that is just audible at a given frequency. The **threshold of feeling** occurs at a high intensity level (approximately 120 dB) and is characterised by a tickling sensation in the ear, which occurs when the ossicles vibrate so strongly that they strike the wall of the middle ear. A sustained noise level above about 85 dB may cause permanent damage to the inner ear. At about

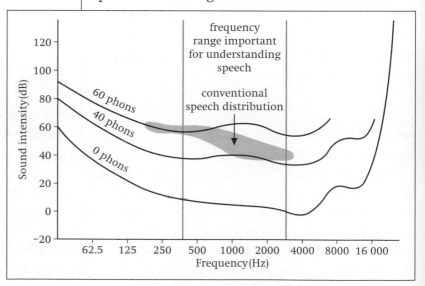

● **Figure 3.5** The standard diagram showing curves of equal loudness at different sound intensity levels for a person with normal hearing.

140 dB, there is a pain threshold and, beyond 160 dB, the eardrum may rupture.

Loudness and intensity level

Loudness and intensity level are not the same quantity, but they are closely related. Intensity level has a distinct, objective, meaning since it is defined against the threshold of hearing, at which no sound is detected by the ear. Loudness depends both on the intensity and on the hearing capability of the observer and is obviously subjective. To overcome this problem, quantitative methods for the **measurement of loudness** have been developed.

In the first method, sounds are compared with a sound of frequency 1000 Hz. The intensity of the 1000 Hz sound is adjusted until it is perceived as being as loud as the sound source being measured. If the intensity level of the 1000 Hz sound is then 50 dB, for example, the second source is said to have a **loudness** of 50 phons. However, this method, known as **phon measurement**, is not easy to carry out in many practical situations.

This has led to the development of several 'weighted' scales of measurement, the A-scale being adopted almost universally; it is denoted dB(A) or, more commonly, dBA. Using this scale, a set of weightings, mimicking the response of the human ear, is applied to measured sound intensity levels at different frequencies, to give curves of equal loudness (figure 3.5). For example, a 60 dB sound will have a loudness of about 40 phons when its frequency is 62.5 Hz and 60 phons when its frequency is 4000 Hz

Hearing defects

The mechanism of hearing can be thought of as a two-stage process. The first stage is through the air (**air conduction**) or possibly through the bone of the skull (**bone conduction**). The second stage is the sensing of vibrations by the neural mechanisms described earlier, starting in the inner ear and finishing in the brain.

If there is a hearing defect in one of the air conductive mechanisms then the result is **conductive deafness**. If there is a defect in the sensory mechanisms of the inner ear the result is **sensorineural deafness**, which may affect only a small band of frequencies. It is possible for both stages to be defective.

Hearing loss is quite common. About 20% of the adult population have hearing that is substantially impaired, i.e. a hearing loss (decrease in intensity level) of 25 dB over the speech range 500–2000 Hz.

The measurement of hearing is called **audiometry**. In an adult audiometry test, sounds at each of six frequencies, 250 Hz, 500 Hz, 1 kHz, 2 kHz, 4 kHz and 8 kHz are used. Air conduction is tested by applying the sound through earphones, while bone conduction is tested using a vibrator in contact with the temporal bone. (The audiometer has been calibrated so that the mean of the intensity levels that can just be heard by a group of young adults with no defect is used as the zero level.) The sound is increased in intensity until the person who is being tested indicates that they can hear it. An audiogram can be plotted (figure 3.6 overleaf), which shows hearing threshold level in decibels against frequency. The graph for a person who has normal hearing would be a straight horizontal line along the zero at the top of the audiogram. For most patients the graph will fall below the zero line. In conductive deafness, sound vibrations do not reach the inner ear. Air conduction is abnormal and bone conduction normal (because the inner ear still works). If there is sensorineural deafness, the hearing either by air conduction or by bone conduction will be measured as abnormal.

Causes of conductive deafness

Conductive deafness could be due to a blockage of the external canal by wax or to puncture or other damage to the eardrum. In the middle ear, the ossicles could be damaged or stiff; if so it is possible to replace them by artificial bones. Temporary conductive deafness can be caused by infection in the middle ear, particularly in children.

Causes of sensorineural deafness

Exposure to excessive noise is the major reason for this type of deafness. Regulations protect workers and where noise levels are above 80 dB employers must make noise-protection equipment available;

if the level is above 90 dB then the employees must wear ear protectors. It should be noted that music played in bars and night clubs is often well above this level.

Other causes of sensorineural deafness include tumours in the brain, viral infections that damage the auditory nerve and congenital defects. An example of the latter is congenital cochlear deafness in a baby, caused when the mother had rubella (German measles) during pregnancy.

Treatment for sensorineural deafness has been impossible until recently. Cochlear implants can now be used to stimulate the auditory nerves with electrical stimuli.

SAQ 3.4

Sounds can be heard by the inner ear when they are transmitted through the bone of the skull. The outer and middle ear play no part in this hearing mechanism. A person suffers hearing loss and it is unclear whether the defect is in the inner ear or the middle ear. Suggest how you could test where the hearing damage has occurred.

Hearing aids

One in four of the population over 65 in the UK experiences some form of hearing loss. This can be remedied, to some extent, by the use of a hearing aid. The normal hearing aid has a microphone connected to an amplifier and then to a loudspeaker. An amplification of 90 dB can be obtained. Even though a deaf person may have a hearing

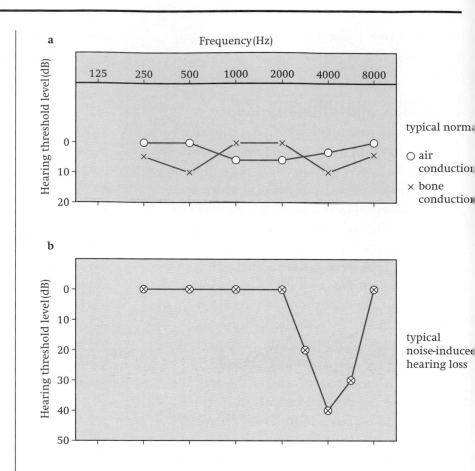

● **Figure 3.6** Audiograms for **a** a person with normal hearing and **b** a person with noise-induced hearing loss.

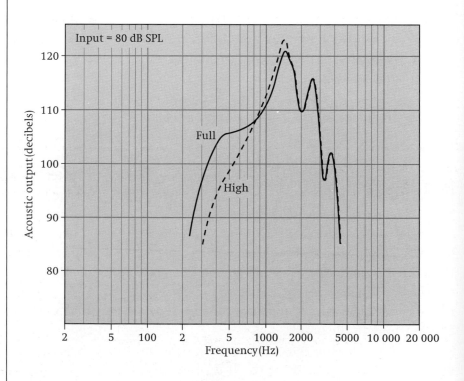

● **Figure 3.7** Frequency response of a hearing aid.

threshold of 70–80 dB, their discomfort threshold is the same as that of a person with normal hearing, i.e. about 100–120 dB. This sets a practical upper limit on the output of the hearing aid. The problem with this simple amplifying system is that it increases all the frequencies that it receives. Normal speech has a range from 400–4000 Hz, but hearing loss normally affects the higher frequencies to a greater extent. If all frequencies are amplified equally, the higher frequencies are boosted to a level where they can now be heard but the amplified low-frequency sounds are too loud (*figure 3.7*).

An attempt is made to overcome this problem in more recent hearing aids. They are very small and can fit into the ear canal. The volume control and switch for the microphone are located on a remote control panel, which is the size of a credit card. A key advantage is that the hearing aid can process each frequency differently. Some frequencies can be amplified while others are decreased.

The latest hearing aids are digital and contain a tiny computer. A mechanism converts sounds into a series of numbers. This information can then be processed by the electronics in the aid. Digital aids have much more flexibility than ordinary analogue aids. They can make it easier to understand speech, even when there is no background noise. However, their main advantage is in fact their ability to reduce background noise, particularly when the user is listening to a conversation. For example, traffic sounds are filtered out.

SUMMARY

- The ear is a transducer. It responds to an incoming sound wave by transmitting the vibrations from the outer ear via the pinna to the ear drum and then via the ossicles to the cochlea, where nerve cells transmit an electrical impulse to the brain. Each of these parts can amplify the intensity.

- The ear responds to a wide range in intensity.

- The frequency response is the smallest percentage change in frequency that the ear can detect.

- The threshold intensity of hearing, I_0, is $10^{-12} \, \text{W m}^2$ at 1000 Hz. Discomfort and damage can occur over about 85 dB.

- The ear has a logarithmic response to intensity.

- Intensity level in decibels = $10 \log_{10} (I/I_0)$.

- Loudness is a subjective response to an intensity level. It is measured in phons.

- Hearing defects can be due to conductive and/or sensorineural deafness.

- Hearing aids amplify the sound received by the ear. Modern digital aids reduce background noise.

Questions

1 Describe the three main parts of the ear and explain their contributions to the process of hearing.

2 a There are two common causes of hearing loss in adults. Explain what these two types are and suggest whether a hearing aid can help these problems.

b A sound of intensity $10^{-6} \, \text{W m}^{-2}$ corresponds to normal conversation. Calculate the sound level in decibels by assuming that the threshold of hearing is $10^{-12} \, \text{W m}^{-2}$.

c To ensure that someone can hear a conversation you raise your voice by 15 dB. Determine the change in sound intensity.

CHAPTER 4

Ionising radiation

By the end of this chapter you should be able to:

1 describe the *microscopic* and *macroscopic* effects, both direct and indirect, of ionising radiation on matter;

2 describe the importance of limiting exposure to ionising radiation;

3 state the difference between the *stochastic* and *non-stochastic* effects of radiation;

4 recall and use the expression $I = I_0 e^{-\mu x}$, which shows how the intensity I of a collimated X-ray beam varies with the thickness x of a medium;

5 distinguish between *exposure* and *absorbed dose*;

6 define and use *absorbed dose* as energy absorbed per unit mass;

7 state that the unit of absorbed dose is a gray (Gy) and calculate values of it;

8 understand that the effect of a given absorbed dose is dependent on the type of ionising radiation;

9 state that equivalent dose in sieverts (Sv) = absorbed dose × quality factor (the quality factor is also known as the radiation weighting factor);

10 describe how absorbed dose is monitored by film badges and thermoluminescent detectors.

By 'ionising radiation' is meant a beam of high-energy particles that will remove one or more electrons from an atom in its path. In chapters 4, 5, 6 and 9, some of the uses of ionising radiation in medicine are considered. X-rays and γ-rays lie at the low-wavelength (high-frequency) end of the electromagnetic spectrum. There is an overlap between the wavelengths of X-rays (10^{-8} to 10^{-13} m) and γ-rays (10^{-10} to 10^{-16} m), the two being the same form of radiation but produced by different mechanisms, as detailed in chapters 5 and 6. Although there is always a benefit to the patient from a diagnostic test or a treatment using ionising radiation, it is important to understand the relatively small risk involved.

Effects of ionising radiation on matter

Ionising radiation causes both **excitation** and **ionisation** of atoms. In ionisation, the atom is separated into two parts with equal and opposite electric charges (a so-called ion pair). The most common ion pair is an electron and the remainder of the atom – a positive ion. In this process, molecular bonds may be broken and abnormal chemical reactions induced, although many such changes are transient and of no biological significance. We shall consider a simple model of a cell. In this model, a cell nucleus containing the DNA – the double helix, deoxyribonucleic acid – is

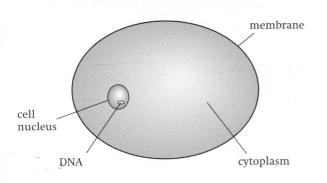

membrane

cell nucleus

DNA

cytoplasm

● **Figure 4.1** Simple model of a cell.

surrounded by **cytoplasm** and enclosed by a **cell membrane** as shown in *figure 4.1*. There are three possible types of **microscopic**, i.e. small-scale, damage process.

- The direct-action mechanism for DNA damage is where the DNA itself absorbs the radiation energy. Permanent changes are known as **mutations**.
- If the ionising event takes place in the cytoplasm (largely water), electrically neutral **free radicals** are produced: a water molecule splits into H· and ·OH. These are highly reactive and can diffuse into the cell nucleus to cause chemical damage to the DNA.
- Damage to the cell membrane itself may cause changes in permeability, affecting the distribution of molecules and ions inside the cell.

Mutations can cause cell death or render a cell sterile, unable to undergo division. They may also lead to large-scale **macroscopic** changes: the uncontrollable growth of a tumour. The sterilisation or killing of a single cell among millions in tissue will have no macroscopic effects. If many cells are affected, however, this may have an effect on tissue function. Such macroscopic effects are known as **non-stochastic** (or **deterministic**); they depend on the number of cells affected and are of particular importance at high radiation doses. It is found that the probability of occurrence of non-stochastic effects is zero below a threshold dose; above this value the probability and severity of the effect increase with dose. This is discussed further on page 40.

At low radiation doses, **stochastic** effects are particularly important. These are random macroscopic events arising from cells that have been damaged but not killed or sterilised, the most important of which is cancer induction. Here, it is assumed that there is no threshold and so no 'safe' radiation dose. The risk becomes progressively lower as radiation dose decreases but never disappears completely. If the unlikely event of cancer induction happens, its consequence will be equally severe whatever the radiation dose.

Effects are classed also as either **somatic**, affecting only the individual irradiated, or **hereditary**, affecting the irradiated person's egg or sperm cells and ultimately their offspring.

Absorption of photons by matter

Unlike charged particles, photons do not directly cause large-scale ionisation of the matter or tissue through which they pass. The energy of the photons is transferred with very low efficiency to kinetic energy in the electrons of the absorbing material and dissipated in further ionisation and excitation.

The absorption of photons is related exponentially to the intensity of the radiation, I, which decreases with thickness of the absorbing material, x, and depends on a constant μ, the **linear attenuation coefficient**, characteristic of the material and of the energy of the photons. The mathematical expression relating I and x is

$$I = I_0 e^{-\mu x}$$

where I_0 is the intensity of the incident ray.

Worked example

For 1 MeV radiation incident on tissue, the linear attenuation coefficient is $7\,\mathrm{m^{-1}}$. Calculate the thickness of tissue required to reduce the intensity of the beam by half.

When $I = I_0/2$, substituting in the above equation we get

$$\tfrac{1}{2} = e^{-\mu x}$$

Thus $e^{\mu x} = 2$

$$\mu x = \log_e 2 = 0.693$$

$$x = \frac{0.693}{7\,\mathrm{m^{-1}}} = 0.1\,\mathrm{m}$$

The value of x in the worked example is the **half-value thickness** in tissue at this photon energy. In lead, the half-value thickness is 7.9×10^{-3} m, which is almost ten times less. This is why lead is used as an absorber.

There are three main processes involved in the absorption of X-ray and γ-ray photons: the photoelectric effect, Compton scattering and pair production, in which a photon, passing through the electric field of a nucleus, is 'catalysed' to become an electron–positron pair. At the photon energies involved in medicine, only the first two processes are important.

Photoelectric effect

In the photoelectric effect, the incident photon ejects one of the orbital electrons from an atom of the absorbing material, giving its energy to the electron. This electron then travels through the absorber ionising and exciting other atoms in the material (*figure 4.2*). An electron from a higher shell may drop down to fill the 'hole' left by the ejected electron, with subsequent emission of a characteristic X-ray photon.

For this process the attenuation coefficient μ increases in proportion to the cube of the atomic number, Z^3, and reduces in proportion to the cube of the incident photon energy, E^3:

$$\mu \propto Z^3$$

$$\mu \propto \frac{1}{E^3}$$

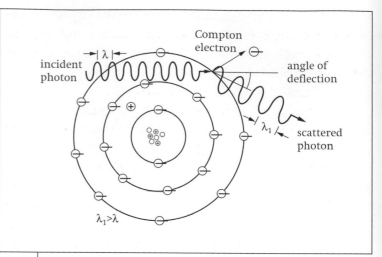

● **Figure 4.3** Compton scattering. The scattered photon has a lower energy than the incident photon and a longer wavelength.

Compton scattering

In Compton scattering, which occurs at higher photon energies, the incident photon is scattered by an orbital electron of an atom in the absorbing material (*figure 4.3*). Some of the photon's energy is given to the electron, which then goes off in a direction different from that of the scattered photon. The electron is called a Compton electron and may have any energy from zero up to a maximum of about two-thirds the incident photon energy. The scattered photon can undergo further scattering processes until finally it is completely absorbed in a photoelectric interaction. For this process the attenuation coefficient μ decreases very gradually with increasing incident photon energy E and is independent of the atomic number Z:

$$\mu \propto \frac{1}{E}$$

As we shall see in chapters 5 and 9, the relative probabilities of photoelectric absorption and Compton scattering determine which radiation energies are best for diagnostic imaging and for radiotherapy.

Radiation measurement

As the ionising radiation interacts with tissue, it causes the formation of ion pairs within a very small volume and so the amount of energy deposited at cellular level

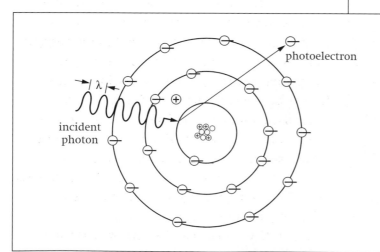

● **Figure 4.2** The photoelectric effect. The incident photon gives up its energy to an orbital electron, which is ejected from the atom.

is very large. This explains the extreme sensitivity of biological tissue to ionising radiation – the amount of energy that would raise the body temperature by 0.003 K if supplied as heat is sufficient to cause death if supplied in the form of γ-radiation.

One of the easiest radiation quantities to measure is **exposure** X, which is defined as the absolute value of the charge of ions of one sign (+ or −) produced in a unit mass of air by a beam of photons:

$$X = \frac{Q}{m}$$

where Q is the charge produced in mass m of air; the SI units of X are C kg^{-1}. The equation is strictly true only for X-rays and γ-rays in air but, since the average atomic number of soft tissue is very close to that of air, the air measurement of X can be used to approximate to its value in soft tissue.

The measurement of the radiation dose given to the tissues of the body is a complex process. It begins with the physical measurement of the amount of energy absorbed per unit mass of tissue, which is known as the **absorbed dose**, D:

$$D = \frac{E}{M}$$

where E is the energy in joules absorbed by a mass M, measured in kilograms. The unit of absorbed dose is the **gray**, which is defined as an absorption of one joule per kilogram (1 Gy = 1 J kg^{-1}). Typical examples of absorbed dose are shown in *table 4.1*.

Absorbed dose can be measured readily, but the biological effects differ for different types of

Procedure	Absorbed dose (Gy)
Chest X-ray	0.0015
Skin dose from CT scan (see page 48)	0.05
γ-ray dose that would just produce reddening of skin	3.0
Absorbed dose to whole body in a short period that would be fatal in half of all cases	5.0
Typical absorbed dose to tumour in course of radiotherapy treatment	60
Absorbed dose to thyroid from iodine-131 given to treat thyrotoxicosis	65

● **Table 4.1** Absorbed dose for some medical procedures.

radiation. Radiation that causes dense ionisation, such as α-particles and neutrons, is termed high linear energy transfer (LET) radiation and is much more damaging than X- or γ-radiation; these are termed low LET radiation. The problem of differing effects is overcome by the introduction of a **quality factor** (**radiation weighting factor**), which is used to 'weight' the absorbed dose. For X-, β- and γ-radiation, the quality factor is 1 and so the equivalent dose is numerically equal to the absorbed dose. For α-particles the quality factor is 20 and for neutrons it is in the range 5–20, depending on their energy.

Using the quality factor, we define a quantity known as the **equivalent dose** to an organ, or a region of the body; the unit of equivalent dose is the **sievert** (symbol Sv). It should be noted this terminology supersedes the term 'dose equivalent', which now refers to the dose supplied at a point. The definition of equivalent dose is as follows:

equivalent dose (Sv) = absorbed dose (Gy)
× quality factor

SAQ 4.1

During radiation testing a health worker is exposed to 10 μGy of α-radiation, with quality factor (radiation weighting factor) equal to 20, and 25 μGy of γ-radiation, with quality factor 1. Calculate the total equivalent dose for these radiations.

The risk of illness and death from radiation depends also on which of the body organs are irradiated; some are more sensitive than others. So that the effects of irradiating different organs can be compared, the concept of the **organ weighting factor** W_t has been developed. These factors have been defined by the International Commission on Radiological Protection and, at present, have the values shown in *table 4.2*. In the table, each item listed in the first column counts as *one organ*, including lungs, breasts, and 'remainder'; the latter quantity refers to the sum of all other organs sensitive to radiation.

A quantity called the **effective dose** is then defined as:

effective dose (Sv) = Σ (organ equivalent dose
× W_t)

Organ	Organ weighting factor W_t
Gonads	0.2
Lungs, red bone marrow, stomach, colon	0.12 (for each organ)
Thyroid, liver, oesophagus, breasts, bladder, remainder	0.05 (for each organ)
Skin, bone surfaces	0.01 (for each organ)

● Table 4.2 Organ weighting factors.

where the symbol Σ means that the product is calculated for all irradiated organs and the answers summed. The effective dose can then be used to predict the risk of fatal cancer, which is presently defined as 5% per sievert. This means that, if 100 people were all exposed to an effective dose of 1 Sv in total then the number of these people who will develop a fatal cancer is most likely to be five.

SAQ 4.2

For a chest X-ray, assume that the approximate equivalent dose to the lungs is 36 µSv, to the red marrow 11 µSv, to the liver 16 µSv and to all other tissues 1 µSv per organ. Calculate the effective dose.

Macroscopic effects

If the radiation dose is received over a short time, no definite health effects should result for effective doses up to 100 µSv and early death is unlikely. At dose levels to a foetus above 100 µSv, there is evidence of mental retardation. For adults receiving a dose between 100 µSv and 2 Sv, increasingly severe effects occur – temporary loss of fertility, decreased white blood cell count, nausea – but recovery is probable. People receiving a dose between 2 and 10 Sv will suffer severe illness and be increasingly unlikely to survive. Doses of 10–20 Sv will cause death within days while 20 Sv or higher will lead to death within a few hours.

For the special category of persons working with ionising radiation, the **maximum permissible radiation dose** to the whole body is 20 mSv per year; the maximum dose allowed to any individual organ is 500 mSv per year, with the exception of the lens of the eye, for which the limit is 150 mSv per year. For a member of the public, the whole body figure is 1 mSv and the individual organ limit is 50 mSv (for the eye lens, 15 mSv).

Background radiation

In the UK, background radiation averages some 2.2 mSv per year. The major natural components arise from radon gas (originating from the radioactive decay of radium in rocks, particularly granite), from cosmic and terrestrial γ-rays and from the naturally occurring radionuclides in our bodies (principally potassium-40 and carbon-14). By far the largest artificial component is due to medical exposure. Approximate annual values are given in *table 4.3*. To put the values in the table into perspective, 1 mSv = 1000 µSv is:

■ the annual dose to the most exposed individuals from the nuclear industry;
■ half the annual dose from natural radiation in the UK (see the first subtotal in the table);
■ 100 times the dose that would be absorbed by flying from the UK to Spain in a jet.

The total amount of background radiation, as can be seen from the table, is 2152 µSv per year, which is just over 2 mSv. Since 1870 µSv is due to natural radiation there is little that we can do about it. The amount of radiation dose from medical uses is expected to decrease since techniques such as ultrasound (see chapter 7) and MRI (see chapter 8) that involve no ionising radiation are increasingly used.

Source	Effective dose (µSv y⁻¹)
Natural	
radon	800
terrestrial γ-rays	400
internal radionuclides	370
cosmic rays	300
subtotal	1870
Artificial	
medical exposure	250
miscellaneous (flight, coal ash, TV etc.)	11
nuclear fallout	10
occupational exposure	9
nuclear power industry waste	2
subtotal	282
Total	2152

● Table 4.3 Breakdown of average UK annual background radiation dose.

Activity	Average risk of death per year
Smoking 10 cigarettes per day	one in 200
Being a man aged 40	one in 500
Road accident	one in 5000
Accident at work	one in 20 000
Medical radiotherapy	one in 250 000

● **Table 4.4** Risks (per year) of death from various causes.

The risk of dying through radiation can be compared with other risks. A man aged 40 has on average a one in 500 chance of dying of natural causes during a year. *Table 4.4* shows the annual risk of dying from various causes.

While the risk from radiation is very small, it is not zero. It is the aim of physicists to reduce that risk by using lower doses of ionising radiation or, as mentioned above, methods that do not involve ionising radiation.

Personal radiation monitoring

There are several different methods by which radiation can be detected. In health physics, however, only a few particular types are useful, because many of the detectors need to be **portable**, and therefore of small size; furthermore, the specific **information** that is required about the radiation limits one's choice of detector.

Film badges

Film badge dosimeters are worn by the great majority of people whose work includes the use of ionising radiation. They provide a relatively cheap and easy method of detecting and measuring the radiation to which such people are exposed over a period of time. The badge is usually worn for a period of 1–4 weeks, after which it is processed. The film is about $3 \times 5 \, \text{cm}^2$ and is contained in a plastic holder that can be pinned to the person's clothing.

A typical badge is shown in *figure 4.4*. A piece of film (see chapter 5, p. 00) is used to detect the different radiations to which the wearer might be exposed. This is achieved by covering the different areas of the film with a series of different

materials, which act as filters. One area has no filters, so that it can measure the total dose.

The film under the plastic windows absorbs differing proportions of different energies of β-particles, depending on the thickness of the plastic. When compared with the unshielded film, both the total amount and the energies of the β-radiation incident on the film can be estimated.

The metal windows absorb β-particles and so prevent them reaching the film. They can be used, therefore, to differentiate between neutrons, and high and low energies of X-rays and γ-rays:

■ the aluminium will absorb low energy X- and γ-rays, but those of higher energy will reach the film;

■ the lead and tin panel will absorb all but the highest energy X- and γ-rays;

■ the lead and cadmium panel will also absorb most X- and γ-rays, but thermal (low energy) neutrons will pass through the lead and interact with the cadmium to produce γ-rays which will blacken this area of the film.

The amount of blackening in each area of the badge depends on the type and energy of the radiation to which the badge has been exposed. It can be accurately calculated using a densitometer,

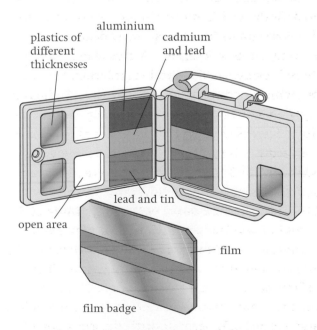

● **Figure 4.4** A film badge dosimeter. The film, wrapped in a light-tight covering, is placed between the two halves of the holder. The dosimeter is worn on the worker's waistband, below protective clothing such as a lab coat.

which measures the amount of light transmitted through each area of the film. The film is double sided, with a fast emulsion on one side to detect small amounts of radiation; on the other side is a slow emulsion that allows higher amounts of radiation to be measured. During processing the fast emulsion is measured first, then stripped away so that the slow emulsion can be measured.

The fast emulsion will absorb and measure radiation doses from $50\,\mu Sv$ to about $50\,mSv$. The slow emulsion will measure up to $10\,Sv$. The film contains an indium panel which can measure doses higher than $10\,mSv$ of thermal neutrons.

Advantages and disadvantages

The advantages of film badge dosimeters are that:
- they are cheap;
- they give a permanent record of the radiation exposure;
- they are easy to use.

The disadvantages are that:
- the accuracy of measurement is only between 10% and 20%;
- the film is affected by temperature and humidity;
- most importantly, the record of radiation is only known some time after the exposure has occurred.

SAQ 4.3

a Describe the key features of the measurement of radiation by film badges.

b Explain in your own words the main disadvantage of monitoring radiation dose by this method.

Thermoluminescent detectors

Radiation can be measured by the **scintillation** (emission of light) that it causes in certain materials. In most cases the light is emitted within fractions of a second after the ionising event. However, **lithium fluoride** is an example of a **thermoluminescent** material, which absorbs the radiation energy by lifting electrons into higher energy levels from which they cannot 'escape'. When additional thermal energy is supplied, the electrons fall back to their original energy levels, giving out light. Lithium fluoride can thus store the information about an accumulated radiation dose until needed, rather like a film badge. So, it has become widely used as a radiation monitoring device.

Either a powder or a 'chip' of material is used, usually sealed in a thin plastic capsule that can be carried on a worker to measure a personal dose or placed on a laboratory wall to measure the radiation dose in a room over a period of time. In order to read out the stored radiation dose, the material is heated to $250\,°C$, which causes the emission of light, the amount being proportional to the radiation dose to which the dosimeter has been exposed. This is measured by a photomultiplier, as described in chapter 6 (page 52). The dosimeter is calibrated against known amounts of radiation so that the dose of radiation received by the dosimeter can be calculated.

There is no permanent record of dose (the reading can be obtained only once), but the device can give a reading as soon as required and can be reused a large number of times. It is more accurate than the film badge and has a sensitivity that varies little with energy. Since it can record a dose of up to $1\,kGy$ (compared to $1\,Gy$ for the film badge), it can also be used to measure patient doses during radiotherapy.

SAQ 4.4

Compare and contrast film badges and thermoluminescent detectors.

SUMMARY

◆ Ionising radiation can cause the excitation and ionisation of matter.

◆ Microscopic damage to cells from radiation can involve mutations, the production of free radicals or damage to the cell membrane.

◆ The macroscopic effects of radiation fall into two categories, stochastic and non-stochastic.

◆ A stochastic event may arise when a cell is damaged but not sterilised. Such an event is random: it cannot be predicted. The effects may be fatal, because of the possibility of cancer, even at low dosages.

◆ Non-stochastic effects of radiation, in which cells are actually sterilised, are important at high radiation doses.

◆ X-ray and γ-ray photons are absorbed by the photoelectric effect and by Compton scattering, at the energies used in medicine.

◆ Exposure X is related to the (+ or −) charge Q produced in mass m of air:
$$X = Q/m$$

◆ Absorbed dose D is energy E deposited per mass M of tissue:
$$D = E/M$$

◆ The unit of absorbed dose is the gray ($1\,\text{Gy} = 1\,\text{J}\,\text{kg}^{-1}$).

◆ The equivalent dose to an organ (measured in sieverts, Sv) is equal to absorbed dose × quality factor (radiation weighting factor).

◆ The dominant contribution to background radiation comes from natural sources.

◆ A film badge is an inexpensive method of recording both the type of radiation and the dose to which the wearer has been exposed. The different types of radiation can be detected by the use of different absorbers in front of the film and the dose by the degree of blackening of the film. While the method is relatively simple, it is not precise and detection takes place some time after the radiation has been absorbed.

◆ Thermoluminescent detectors use the scintillator lithium fluoride. They can give a reading at any time, on being heated, and can be reused.

Questions

1 A health physicist works with several different sources of radiation during a year. He receives 250 μGy from neutrons with a quality factor (radiation weighting factor) of 10, and 3 mGy from a γ-ray source, for which the quality factor is 1. Calculate the equivalent dose for the year.

2 In the preparation of radioactive sources the regulations state that no worker should receive more than 20 mSv per year. During the preparation of radiopharmaceuticals, a health worker receives an estimated absorbed dose of $5 \times 10^{-6}\,\text{Gy}$ from each source. The quality factor (radiation weighting factor) is 1. During a year 3000 sources are prepared by this worker. Show by calculation whether the recommended level is exceeded.

CHAPTER 5

Radiology: X-rays in diagnosis

By the end of this chapter you should be able to:

1 describe in simple terms the need for *non-invasive* techniques in diagnosis;

2 understand the nature of *X-rays* and give a simple explanation of their production;

3 understand the relative importance of the photoelectric effect and Compton scattering in *attenuating* an X-ray beam;

4 describe the use of X-rays in *imaging* internal body structure, including their use in *image intensifiers* and with *contrast media*;

5 describe how a *computed tomography* (CT) scanner operates.

Non-invasive techniques

In hospitals, a large amount of time and money is spent on producing medical images of various types. A typical hospital will generate over half a million images a year. Worldwide, the number of images produced in medicine comes second only to that produced by satellites. The most common technique for producing images is still radiology, but other techniques such as nuclear medicine, ultrasound, magnetic resonance imaging (MRI), thermography and fibre optic probes are increasingly now used.

These techniques are described as **non-invasive** since, apart from some uses of fibre optic probes, they do not require surgery on the patient to produce the image. This means that there is a much lower risk to the patient. Also, there are fewer medical difficulties and less expense. Some techniques make use of radiation, either transmitted through the patient from an external source (X-rays or ultrasound) or emitted from within the patient, naturally (thermography) or from an internal source (nuclear medicine). Some techniques will involve 'perturbing' the body system, for example where a contrast medium is injected to make the structures in the image clearer or where the patient takes exercise, as in studies of the heart and circulatory system.

In this chapter we will consider **radiology**, the use of X-rays in diagnosis.

The production of X-rays

X-rays are electromagnetic waves above ultraviolet frequencies, i.e. with wavelengths in the range 10^{-8}–10^{-13} m. They were discovered by Wilhelm Röntgen in 1895. In a modern **X-ray tube** a high voltage, about 100 kV, is placed across electrodes in an evacuated tube (*figure 5.1*). When the

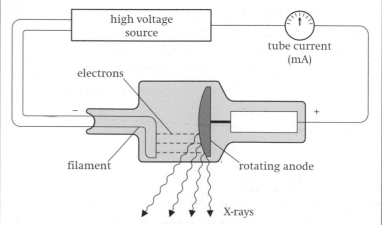

● **Figure 5.1** Schematic diagram of an X-ray tube.

negative electrode (cathode) is heated by an electric current passing through it, electrons are emitted. These electrons are accelerated by the high voltage to hit the positive electrode (anode). When the electrons strike the anode, most of their energy is transferred into thermal energy. However, some of the energy causes the emission of X-rays. The greater the voltage across the electrodes, the greater the energy of the X-rays. The energy of a photon is related to the frequency as follows:

$$E = hf$$

where h (Planck's constant) $= 6.63 \times 10^{-34}$ J s. Hence, as the energy increases, the frequency f of the X-rays increases and the wavelength decreases.

To produce X-rays for use in diagnosis, the voltage across the electrodes is held between 80 and 120 kV. For treatment of cancers, the voltage used is greater than 200 kV, to produce X-rays of greater energy. X-ray photons are produced by two processes when a fast-moving stream of electrons is rapidly decelerated in a material of high atomic number.

- **Characteristic X-rays**, which have definite energies, are produced when there is a rearrangement of the electrons within a target atom following the removal of an inner-shell electron. These are relatively unimportant in medical applications.
- **Bremsstrahlung (braking radiation)** is associated with the deflections of a bombarding electron in the electrostatic fields of the target nuclei. Since it is likely that in each deflection only a fraction of the electron's energy will be transferred, bremsstrahlung X-rays have a continuous range of energies, the maximum being the energy of the bombarding electrons (i.e. when all the energy is transferred to one photon). The composite output spectrum from a typical X-ray tube is shown in *figure 5.2*.

A basic X-ray system is shown in *figure 5.3*.

X-ray attenuation

The various processes by which X-ray photons are absorbed, i.e. the photoelectric effect, Compton scattering and pair production, were described

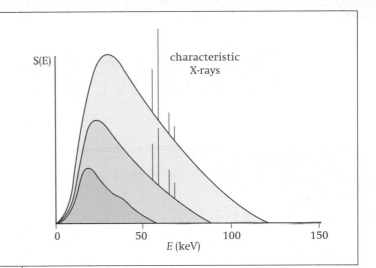

● **Figure 5.2** X-ray spectra for a tungsten target with accelerating voltages of 60, 90 and 120 kV. The peaks correspond to characteristic X-rays and the continuous curves to the bremsstrahlung component. Note that at low values of accelerating voltage the electrons do not have enough energy to produce characteristic X-rays. For each curve the *maximum* X-ray energy equals the kinetic energy of the electrons.

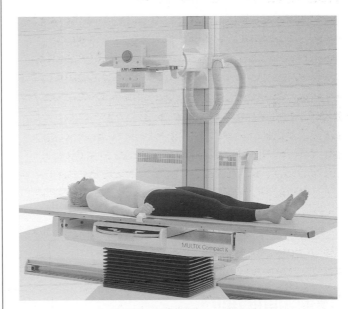

● **Figure 5.3** A general-purpose X-ray system.

briefly in chapter 4. Because of this absorption, X-rays are **attenuated** as they pass through matter. The attenuation coefficient μ is defined by the equation

$$I = I_0 e^{-\mu x}$$

For the photoelectric effect, μ is proportional to Z^3/E^3. For Compton scattering, μ is proportional to $1/E$ and does not depend on Z.

The dependence of μ on atomic number Z has significance when X-ray photons strike tissue. Soft tissue has an average atomic number of 7 because it contains the light elements carbon, hydrogen and oxygen. Bone, however, has an effective atomic number of 14 due to the high proportions of calcium and phosphorus in it. Since photoelectric absorption increases in proportion to Z^3, this effect is much more likely to occur in bone than in soft tissue. The photoelectric effect is therefore much more useful than Compton scattering since it allows us to see bones and other heavy materials in the body: bone appears more opaque than soft tissue, in X-ray images.

In order to ensure that photoelectric absorption is the dominant process, it is necessary to operate at low energies, since the probability of absorption is dependent on E^{-3}. At 30 keV, bone absorbs X-rays eight times better than tissue.

If Compton scattering was the only process that could be used, then X-rays would have limited usefulness since for Compton scattering the only distinction between bone and tissue is that bone has a greater density of scatterers. Bone has about twice the density of tissue and so will be seen on an X-ray image, but with low contrast. The Compton effect can also reduce the information on an X-ray image because it gives rise to scattered photons, which reduce the detail on the image.

SAQ 5.1

In medical diagnosis, in which kind of case would X-rays produce good images?

X-ray detection

Like photographic film, an X-ray film consists of an inert plastic sheet coated with silver halide crystals. On absorption of radiation, the silver halide molecules become ionised; processing (developing and fixing) turns the silver ions into black silver particles to produce an image. The relationship between the degree of blackening (optical density) and exposure to X-rays is shown in *figure 5.4*. This is known as the **characteristic curve** of the film.

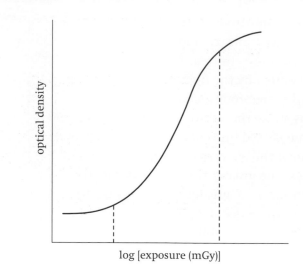

● **Figure 5.4** Characteristic curve for X-ray film.

The film is relatively insensitive since most X-rays will pass through it without interaction. It can be made to record more of the X-rays if it is sandwiched between two sheets each containing a phosphor; this converts X-rays to visible light, to which the film is more sensitive. Each X-ray photon produces several thousand light photons, though only 10%–20% of these are detected. Such **intensifier screens** permit an image to be obtained with 100–500 times less exposure to radiation.

In digital X-ray detection systems, the most common arrangement is for the X-ray beam to be directed on to an **image intensifier** (*figure 5.5*). This comprises a fluorescent screen (phosphor) backed by a photocathode. When the X-ray photons hit the screen, the energy is converted first into light photons and then electrons. These electrons are accelerated and focussed by an electric field on to a smaller fluorescent screen within the anode, which is viewed by a television camera. This information is fed into a computer.

Contrast media

Conventional radiography is based upon the differential attenuation of X-rays by the different tissues of the body. The differing amounts of radiation reaching the film or detector are recorded and form an image. As noted above, low energy X-rays are used for diagnostic imaging, since at low energies the photoelectric effect dominates. Because several types of soft body tissue have

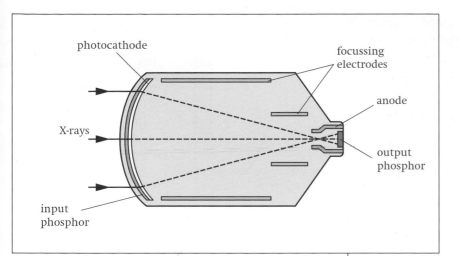

● **Figure 5.5** Schematic diagram of an image intensifier. The broken lines represent the electrons into which the X-rays are indirectly converted.

almost the same average atomic number, they produce very little difference in attenuation. So, on the final image, there is little contrast between them to make them visible. In such cases, **contrast media** are used. These are usually materials of very high atomic number, such as iodine and barium; as we have seen, these exhibit large X-ray absorption. Liquids containing iodine can be injected into selected blood vessels to study blood flow, and barium can be swallowed to outline the stomach and intestines (*figure 5.6*).

Digital systems are used in radiography primarily in subtraction techniques in which an image of a structure, such as the arrangement of blood vessels in the kidney, is compared with another image of the same structure after injection with a contrast medium. The first image is subtracted from the second to give a resulting image that contains details only of the blood vessels carrying the contrast medium (*figure 5.7*). This is a very powerful technique and permits the imaging of small structures. Modern computing techniques can even correct for motion of the patient between the two images.

Therapeutic use

Digital X-ray systems are employed also for therapeutic purposes. An example of this is **balloon angioplasty**, in which a catheter (a narrow hollow tube) is inserted into an artery in the thigh and passed back into a narrowed artery in the heart or elsewhere. The contrast medium is injected and the position of the blockage in the artery is established. An inflatable balloon is then positioned inside the blockage under X-ray control and blown

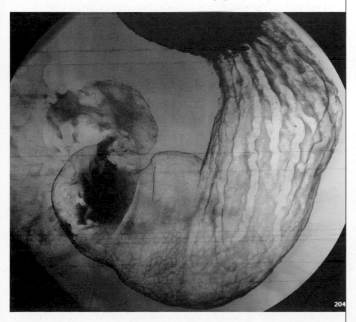

● **Figure 5.6** Contrast X-ray of intestinal tract. The liquid has coated the wall of the tract, enabling its outline to be seen. The remaining liquid can be seen further down the tract at the lower left of the image.

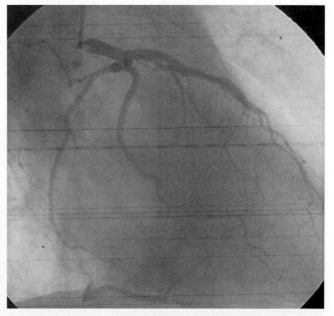

● **Figure 5.7** Digital subtraction image of blood vessels in the brain. Structures such as the bones are cancelled out in the final image, which shows the contrast material passing through the blood vessels.

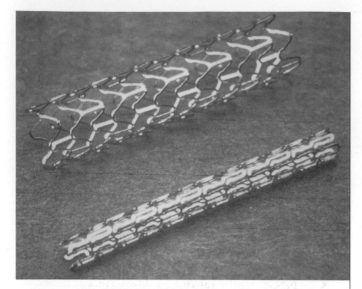

● **Figure 5.8** A stent is sometimes used in angioplasty: before insertion it is collapsed (bottom); the stent is expanded to hold the artery open (top).

up, compressing the material blocking the artery and widening the opening for blood to flow through; the balloon is then deflated and removed. As an alternative, a **stent** (*figure 5.8*) can be placed inside the narrowed section, opened out and left in place (*figure 5.9*).

Computed tomography

Conventional X-ray photographs, or radiographs, are the most common images used in hospitals. However, they have an important limitation – they contain superimposed information from all depths in the body. One possible solution is to use a rotating beam and take a number of X-rays from

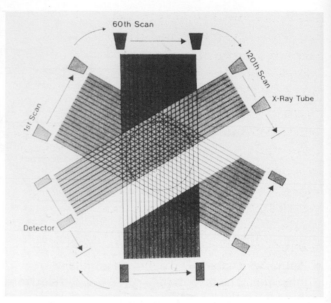

● **Figure 5.10** Operation of the first-generation CT scanners. An X-ray tube and a single detector opposite to it were mounted on a gantry. After each scan the gantry was rotated a few degrees to a new position.

different angles; from these the radiologist can work out which parts of the image correspond to which part of each organ. This is a rather difficult and time-consuming process.

In 1971 Geoffrey Hounsfield and his colleagues at EMI (Electrical and Musical Instruments Ltd) in the UK developed a machine to overcome these problems, the **computerised axial tomographic scanner** (CAT or CT) scanner. The mode of operation of the first scanner is shown in *figure 5.10*. An X-ray tube and detector were mounted on a gantry that was free to scan across and around the patient. A narrow, pencil-thin, X-ray beam was used to obtain the finest detail. At each position, a measurement of the amount of radiation transmitted through the patient was made. Each scan was made by moving the tube and detector through a series of such positions (*figure 5.10*). The gantry was then rotated by a few degrees. The process was repeated until the machine had made one complete revolution of the patient.

These early scanners showed that the technique could work

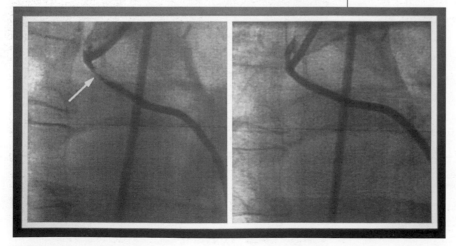

● **Figure 5.9** Angiogram before (left) and after (right) stent insertion; the narrowed section of the artery (white arrow) is now held fully open.

but it took 10–15 minutes to complete each 'slice'. In the very first scans, the patient had to be surrounded by water-filled bags to make the length of material through which the X-ray beam passed equal in all directions. The computer
program used to reconstruct the data can now correct for differing path lengths. The reconstruction process normally used is called **filtered back projection**.

Modern scanners can collect the data in a few seconds. **Fourth-generation** scanners (*figure 5.11*) use a fan-shaped X-ray beam (collimated to be very narrow in the longitudinal direction, perpendicular to the plane of the diagram) and a complete ring of up to 1000 individual detectors; in these machines, only the X-ray tube rotates around the patient. The leading and trailing edges of the fan beam are outside the patient and so can be used to calibrate the detectors during the scan. Various detectors can be used, such as sodium iodide scintillation crystals, the semiconductor bismuth germanate or xenon ionisation chambers.

In a **fifth-generation** system, the patient's bed moves longitudinally through the gantry as the X-ray tube rotates. This means that the X-ray beam effectively describes a spiral path around the patient and information about a whole volume is obtained.

Since the image will be fuzzy if there is movement during a scan, the patient is requested to hold his or her breath.

Advantages of CT scanners

CT scanners can produce three-dimensional information that shows quite small differences in tissue density and also the depth of the particular structure (*figure 5.12*). CT scans can also be produced very quickly. A typical example of their use would be to determine the precise location of a head injury following a traffic or a sporting accident. In such cases the exact position of the injury has to be determined quickly. Other possible cases are where the treatment of a brain

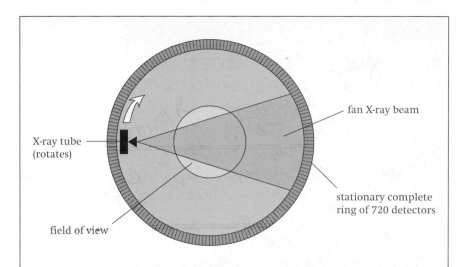

● **Figure 5.11** Operation of a modern CT scanner. Only the X-ray tube moves, making one complete revolution. The X-ray beam has a fan shape, so that many measurements can be made simultaneously by a ring of stationary detectors.

tumour involves the precise location and size of the tumour. Again a conventional X-ray would not provide this kind of detailed information.

SAQ 5.2

What are the main advantages of computed tomography in comparison with conventional X-rays?

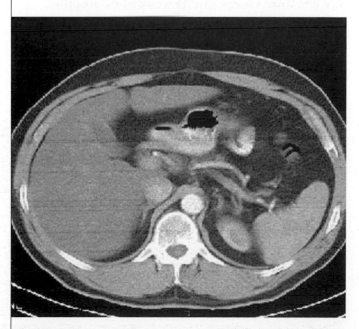

● **Figure 5.12** A CT scan of the abdomen. Lower-density structures appear darker and bone appears lighter.

SUMMARY

◆ Non-invasive techniques in diagnosis are important since the risk to the patient is much lower, the procedures are less difficult and less expensive.

◆ X-rays are produced by a high voltage across a pair of electrodes in a vacuum tube. When electrons strike the anode, X-rays are produced.

◆ X-ray machines are operated at low energies so that the attenuation of the X-rays is mainly by the photoelectric effect. This effect is much greater for bone than for soft tissue, so giving a good contrast between bone and soft tissue in X-ray images.

◆ X-rays can be detected by photographic film. To reduce the exposure of people to radiation, image intensifiers are used.

◆ Contrast media enable different tissues with the same average atomic number Z to be distinguished.

◆ CT scanners operate by a series of X-rays taken as the machine rotates around the patient. A large number of measurements are taken which are processed by a computer to give an image. The main advantage of this technique is to give the image in three dimensions and with greater detail than is possible with a simple X-ray system.

Question

A child is injured in a car crash and experiences pains in the head. There are no obvious signs of head injury but the doctors suggest a CT scan is taken. Explain why this is desirable and what additional information would be obtained.

CHAPTER 6

Diagnostic nuclear medicine

By the end of this chapter you should be able to:

1 describe how the radioactive isotope *technetium-99m* is used for diagnostic purposes;

2 describe how technetium-99m is produced;

3 describe how a scintillation counter operates;

4 describe the structure and typical uses of a gamma camera.

Nuclear medicine

By **nuclear medicine** is meant the use of radioactive materials in medicine, both for diagnosis and therapy. The materials used are **radiopharmaceuticals**, which comprise **pharmaceuticals** (chemicals used in medicine) and a **radionuclide**. The pharmaceutical used will depend on the organ to be studied, while the radionuclide is either the marker (in diagnosis) or the 'warhead' (in therapy).

In **therapy**, the aim is to deposit the radioactive material at the diseased cells so that they will be killed by the radiation. Since the normal cells surrounding the diseased tissue must not be killed, short-range radiations (alpha and beta) are used. This is discussed further in chapter 9.

In **diagnosis**, radioactive materials are used to study the functioning of organs. This is the subject of the present chapter. For diagnostic purposes, the radionuclide needs to be a gamma emitter, because gamma rays are hardly absorbed by the body and can be monitored from outside the patient. The source should have a reasonably short **half-life** to limit the time during which there is a (small) radiation dose to the patient and staff. The radionuclide most commonly used is technetium-99m ('m' means metastable); gamma rays are emitted by this nucleus as it decays to the nucleus technetium-99.

Technetium-99m

If the radionuclide had a long half-life, the patient and others would be subjected to a continuing radiation dose. As mentioned above, a short half-life, such as the six-hour half-life of technetium-99m, limits the radiation dose but could give problems because of the time required to transport the radionuclide from production site to hospital. However, technetium-99m derives from a long-lived 'parent' radionuclide, molybdenum-99. This can be used for the transportation stage; it decays to technetium-99m ready for use with patients. An easy way to separate the two is needed, so that the patient does not receive any of the parent radionuclide.

Molybdenum-99 decays to technetium-99m by beta emission with a half-life of 67 hours and is obtained from a nuclear reactor. The molybdenum-99 is transported to the hospital in a **generator** (*figure 6.1 overleaf*). This comprises a saline reservoir, an alumina column on to which the molybdenum has been adsorbed and a filter. The column is shielded with lead or depleted uranium to reduce the radiation dose to the user.

Procedure

Saline solution is passed through the column; the technetium, which is being produced by beta decay of the molybdenum, is soluble in saline but the

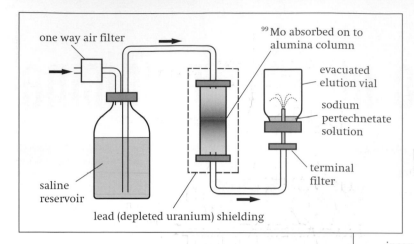

one way air filter

^{99}Mo absorbed on to alumina column

evacuated elution vial

sodium pertechnetate solution

terminal filter

saline reservoir

lead (depleted uranium) shielding

● **Figure 6.1** Schematic diagram of a generator in which technetium-99m, used in diagnosis, is separated from its parent nucleus molybdenum-99. An evacuated collection vial on the output side draws saline from the reservoir through the column. Here the saline dissolves the technetium to form a solution of sodium pertechnetate. This passes through a sterilising filter into the collection vial.

molybdenum itself is not. This process is known as **elution** and results in a solution of sodium pertechnetate, which is collected in an output vial. The contents of the output vial can be diluted and split into a number of **patient doses**. The total amount of radioactivity available is governed by the half-life of molybdenum. The generator is eluted daily until the radioactive concentration falls to a level that is too low to be useful, which happens after two or three half-lives (i.e. 2×67 or 3×67 hours). This means that weekly delivery of a generator to hospital departments is necessary.

SAQ 6.1

a What are the advantages of using technetium–99m as a radioactive isotope in diagnosis?

b Why is the design of the generator useful for a number of patients?

Scintillation detectors

Some materials, when they absorb ionising radiation, produce photons of light. These materials are called **scintillators**. The light is emitted in a short pulse or flash and the amplitude of the pulse depends on the energy absorbed. If a material of high atomic number is used, the sensitivity to small amounts of radiation is increased. The most common scintillator is thallium-activated sodium iodide, NaI(Tl). The light is converted into an electrical signal by a device called a **photomultiplier** (*figure 6.2*).

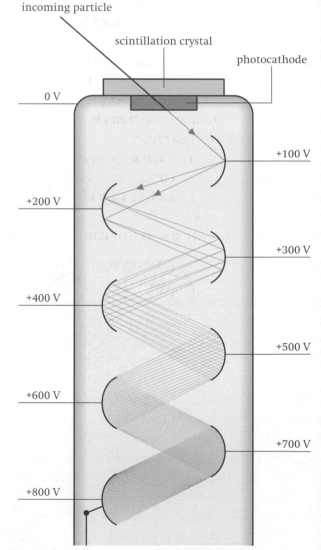

incoming particle

scintillation crystal

photocathode

0 V

+100 V

+200 V

+300 V

+400 V

+500 V

+600 V

+700 V

+800 V

● **Figure 6.2** A scintillation counter showing a cascade of electrons in a photomultiplier. The incoming particle causes the scintillator to emit photons. These in turn cause the emission of electrons from the photocathode. The electrons are accelerated towards the first electrode; there, each electron produces two or three secondary electrons. The process is repeated and soon there is a cascade of electrons, giving a large output pulse.

The gamma camera

The gamma camera (*figure 6.3*) was first developed in 1957 by Hal Anger in the United States. It is the major imaging device in use now in diagnostic nuclear medicine. The camera uses a single, very large sodium iodide crystal, typically between 400 and 500 mm in diameter and 9–12 mm thick. This crystal is viewed by a large number of photo-multipliers arranged in concentric hexagonal rings around a central tube (*figure 6.4*). The field of view is limited by a collimator, consisting of a block of lead that has up to 35 000 holes (*figure 6.5*). The usual parallel-hole collimator allows only photons that travel perpen-dicular to the crystal to pass through.

A gamma photon reaching the scintillator crystal may interact to give a light flash, which will be detected by the photomultipliers. The intensity of light reaching a given photomultiplier will be inversely related to the square

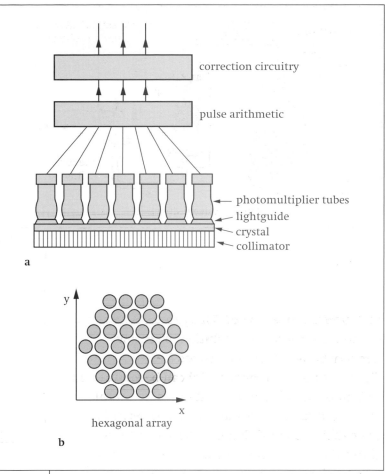

a

b

hexagonal array

● **Figure 6.4** Arrangement of photomultipliers in a gamma camera. **a** Schematic cross-section; **b** plan view.

of its distance from the point of interaction. So, by comparing the differing amplitudes of signals from all the photomultipliers in each of the x- and y-directions, it is possible to work out where in the crystal the light pulse originated. By adding all the photomultiplier outputs a total signal is obtained that depends on the energy of the gamma photon.

It is usual to analyse the energy signal in order to select events corresponding to photoelectric absorption only. Signals corresponding to Compton scattering are rejected because the pho-ton detected by the camera would have originated at the site of the scattering event, replacing the first photon, which came from the site of uptake of the radiopharmaceutical. If this signal were accepted, an incorrect location would be recorded.

For signals corresponding to photoelectric absorption, the position coordinates of the event generate a dot on an oscilloscope. An image of the

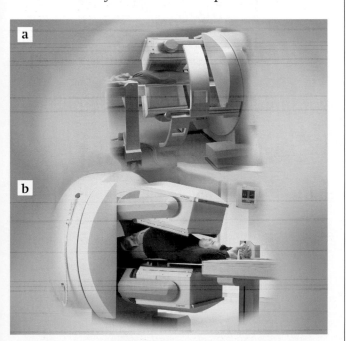

a

b

● **Figure 6.3** A gamma camera. One of the detectors is above the patient, the other is opposite the camera. In this machine the detectors can be either **a** 90° or **b** 180° apart. The former setting is used for emission tomography of the heart; the latter setting is used for planar studies such as the bone scan shown in *figure 6.6*.

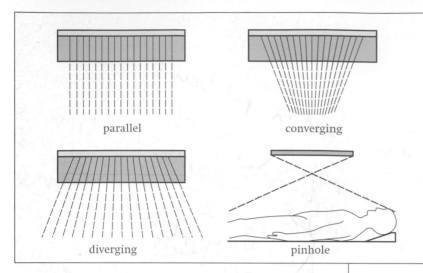

parallel

converging

diverging

pinhole

● **Figure 6.5** Various collimator types. The parallel-hole collimator is the one used most often. The converging collimator magnifies the image of smaller organs, for example parts of the brain, while the diverging collimator allows imaging of organs that are larger than the field of view of the detector. The pinhole can be used to magnify very small organs, such as the thyroid, or to 'minify' a large area, such as the whole body, depending on whether the object is close to or far from the collimator.

distribution of radioactive material in the body is obtained by making a time-exposure photograph of the oscilloscope. This usually contains between 2×10^5 and 5×10^5 dots.

Different collimators can be used with different numbers and sizes of holes (*figure 6.5*). A smaller number of larger holes will increase the **sensitivity** (the fraction of gamma rays from the patient that are detected) but also will reduce the definition, i.e. the ability to see detail. The thickness of the collimator can also affect the sensitivity.

An alternative, more recent, means of storing the data is to send information about the *x* and *y* coordinates of each event directly to a computer, to generate a digital image, rather than a photograph, which can then be processed.

Uses of the gamma camera

The gamma camera can be used in two different types of study:

■ **static study**, in which there is a time delay between injecting the radioactive material into the body and obtaining the images;

■ **dynamic study**, in which the amount of

radiation in an organ is measured as a function of time by taking a series of images, usually starting as the radioactive material is injected.

An example of a static study is a **bone scan**. The radiopharmaceutical consists of a phosphate compound labelled with technetium-99m. Bone scans can be used to detect the spread of cancer into the skeleton. If bone is affected, there will be a high rate of local phosphate metabolism, an increased uptake of the injected phosphate and so a rise in the concentration of the radionuclide. The resulting 'hot-spots' on the image (*figure 6.6*) show the sites of cancer spread, which can be treated by radiotherapy (chapter 9).

An example of a dynamic study is a **renogram**, which examines the function of the kidneys. In this case, a radioactive chemical is chosen which is normally extracted from the bloodstream by the kidneys within a few minutes. If a kidney is functioning correctly then ten to fifteen minutes after administration most of the material should have gone through it to the bladder. The gamma camera is used to measure the radioactivity in the

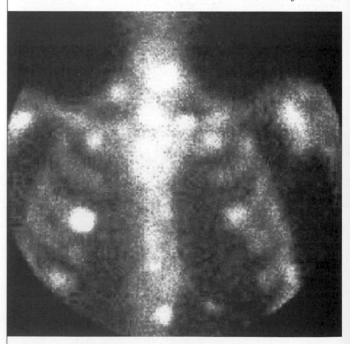

● **Figure 6.6** Bone scan. Areas of high uptake of the radiopharmaceutical reveal regions of high metabolic activity; metastases (secondary tumours) from a cancer appear as hot spots on the image.

kidneys every 20–30 seconds for about 20 minutes, and the data is sent to a computer. The computer will produce a graph of activity (particle emission rate) against time.

SAQ 6.2

Look at the renogram in *figure 6.7*, which shows the radioactivity in the left and right kidneys in a patient after the administration of a radiopharmaceutical. Which kidney is not functioning correctly, and what is the evidence for this?

Modern gamma cameras utilise two (or sometimes three) detectors. In the twin-detector version, the detectors are usually placed 180° apart, permitting images to be obtained simultaneously from both sides of the body. Cross-sectional images of the distribution of the radiopharmaceutical in the body can be produced by rotating the camera around the patient to obtain planar images from a number of different angles (usually 64 or 128). These data are then processed by the computer in a manner analogous to the CT scanner to produce a three-dimensional image (*figure 6.8*). This technique is known as single-photon-emission computed tomography (SPECT).

Positron emission tomography

It is possible to use the twin-detector system to image positron-emitting radiopharmaceuticals.

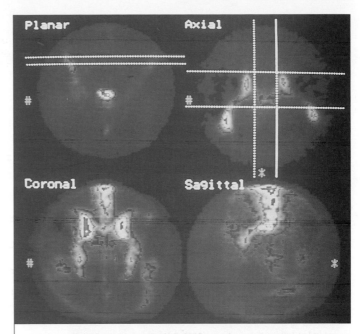

● **Figure 6.8** SPECT bone images.

When a positron annihilates with an electron in tissue, two γ-photons are emitted, in opposite directions, each with an energy of 511 keV. If each detector simultaneously gives a signal corresponding to the detection of a 511 keV photon, the site of the annihilation event must lie along a line joining the two detection sites. By feeding information about a large number of such events into the computer, as the detectors rotate to various positions around the patient, three-dimensional images of the radiopharmaceutical distribution can be obtained; this is positron emission tomography (PET). In purpose-built PET systems, the patient is surrounded by a stationary ring of scintillation detectors, giving a much higher detection efficiency. PET systems are used to image physiologically important processes such as glucose metabolism, for which the radiopharmaceutical ^{18}F-fluorodeoxyglucose is administered to the patient (*figure 6.9* overleaf).

SAQ 6.3

The above techniques use scintillation devices.

a What is meant by a scintillation device?

b Explain what effect the number of holes in a collimator can have on the final image.

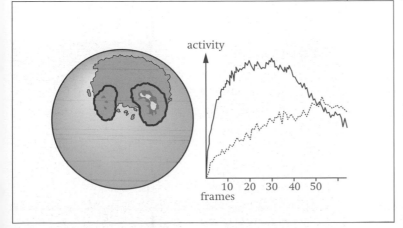

● **Figure 6.7** An image from a renogram series; the operator has outlined the positions of the kidneys (left kidney on the left-hand side). The graph shows the radioactivity in the kidneys as a function of time. The black and dotted lines show the radioactivity in the right and left kidneys respectively.

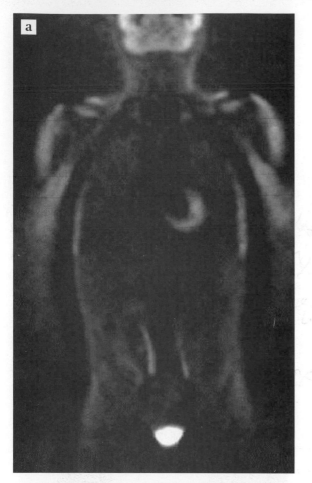

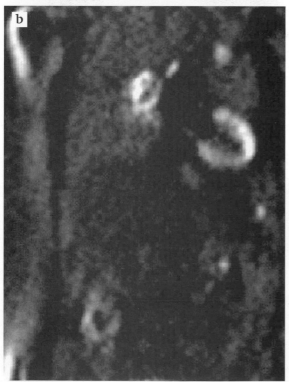

● **Figure 6.9** Images of the whole-body distribution of ^{18}F-fluorodeoxyglucose. **a** normal image, with uptake in the heart and muscles; **b** additional hot spots due to lung cancer tumours.

SUMMARY

◆ Radiopharmaceuticals are used in nuclear medicine for diagnosis and therapy.

◆ Short-range radiations are chosen for therapeutic use.

◆ Technetium-99m is suitable for diagnostic use because it is a gamma emitter having a short half-life.

◆ A generator that each week can produce doses for a number of patients uses the technetium-99m produced by decay of molybdenum-99.

◆ The gamma camera detects gamma rays, originating from a radionuclide introduced into a patient, by means of the scintillator NaI(Tl).

◆ Scintillator flashes are detected by an array of photomultiplier tubes.

◆ Gamma cameras are used in static and dynamic studies.

◆ Modern gamma cameras use more than one crystal detector.

◆ Positron emitters can also be used as radionuclides, since by annihilation with an electron they produce a gamma ray pair.

Question

In nuclear medicine, gamma radiation is used to detect whether an organ is functioning normally.
a Why is this type of radiation used?
b What would be a suitable choice of half-life? Give reasons for your answer.

CHAPTER 7

Ultrasound

By the end of this chapter you should be able to:

1 explain how ultrasonic waves are produced and detected by *piezoelectric transducers*;

2 describe how ultrasonic echosounding can be used to obtain images inside the body;

3 understand the importance of *acoustic impedance* and its dependence on the density of the medium and on wave speed;

4 understand why a coupling medium is required for effective ultrasound techniques;

5 distinguish between A and B scans;

6 understand the principles of Doppler scans.

Production of ultrasound

The normal range of hearing is from 20 to 20 000 Hz and sound-wave frequencies above this range are called **ultrasonic**. Typical frequencies used in medicine are in the megahertz range. Ultrasonic waves cannot produce ionisation and so there is no radiation dose to the patient.

Ultrasonic waves are emitted from a **transducer**, which is a device that changes energy from one form to another. In this case, the transducer is a crystal that exhibits the **piezoelectric** effect: when a potential difference (p.d.) is placed across the crystal it expands along one axis, and when the potential difference is reversed the crystal contracts. If an alternating potential difference that matches the resonant frequency of the crystal is used, the crystal will oscillate rather like the cone of a loudspeaker (*figure 7.1*). The reverse process is also true: if pressure is applied to the crystal, a small potential difference is formed across it. A piezoelectric transducer may thus act both as a **transmitter** and as a **receiver** of ultrasound. The optimum size for the crystal is $\lambda/2$, where λ is the wavelength emitted.

The structure of the transducer has certain key components (*figure 7.2 overleaf*). The outer case

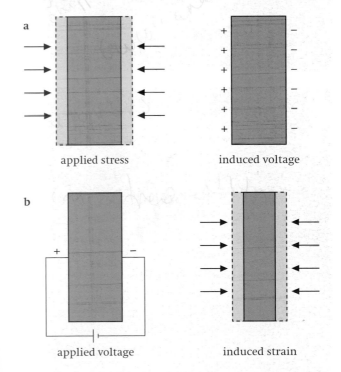

applied stress · induced voltage · applied voltage · induced strain

● **Figure 7.1** The piezoelectric effect. **a** An applied stress causes an induced voltage across the crystal; **b** an applied voltage causes an induced strain.

supports and protects the crystal. The face is a protective **acoustic window**, designed to match the electrical characteristics of the crystal and transmit the ultrasound. It is important that the crystal ceases to vibrate as soon as the alternating

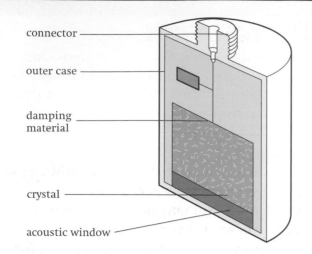

● **Figure 7.2** Section through an ultrasonic transducer.

p.d. stops, so that it is ready to receive the reflected pulse. Therefore a **damping material** (usually epoxy resin) is included above the crystal. Various materials have been used for the crystal, including quartz and lead zirconate titanate. Modern systems use polyvinylidine difluoride.

Echosounding

The basic ultrasound system works on a pulse echo technique using the equation

$$s = vt$$

where s is the distance from the transducer to the object and back, v is the speed of sound and t is the time for the sound to travel to the object and return. If the speed of sound in the different substances between the transducer and object is known and the time interval between pulse and reflected signal can be measured, then the distance travelled by the pulse can be calculated.

When a sound wave strikes a boundary between two substances, some of the energy will be reflected and some will be refracted (*figure 7.3*). The amount of refraction will depend on the **acoustic impedance** of each material, which is given the symbol Z and is defined as:

$$Z = \rho v$$

where ρ is the density of the substance and v is the speed of sound in

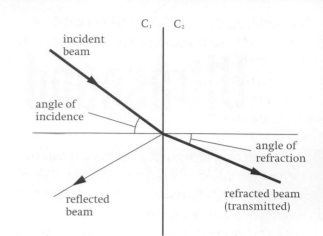

● **Figure 7.3** Behaviour of an ultrasonic beam at a boundary between two tissues, C_1 and C_2. The angle of refraction depends on the ratio of the speed of sound in the two media. The proportion of energy transmitted depends on the acoustic impedances of the two media.

the substance. The greater the difference in acoustic impedance Z between the two materials, the greater is the reflected portion of the incident pulse. It can be shown that for normal incidence the ratio of the reflected intensity I_r to the initial intensity I_0 is given by

$$\frac{I_r}{I_0} = \frac{(Z_2 - Z_1)^2}{(Z_2 + Z_1)^2}$$

where Z_1 is the acoustic impedance of material 1 and Z_2 is that of material 2.

Information about different substances and their acoustic impedances is given in *table 7.1*. Using the above equation, we can deduce ratios of intensities from the Z-values:
for an air–fat boundary, $I_r / I_0 = 0.99$;
for a fat–muscle boundary, $I_r / I_0 = 0.01$;
for a muscle–bone boundary, $I_r / I_0 = 0.41$.

Material	Speed of sound $(\mathrm{m\,s^{-1}})$	Density $(\mathrm{kg\,m^{-3}})$	Acoustic impedance Z $(\mathrm{kg\,m^{-2}\,s^{-1}} \times 10^6)$
Air	330	1.3	0.0004
Bone (adult)	2700–4100	$(1.3$–$1.9) \times 10^3$	7.8
Muscle	1545–1630	1.0×10^3	1.7
Soft tissue	1460–1615	1.0×10^3	1.6
Fat	1450	1.0×10^3	1.4
Blood	1570	1.0×10^3	1.6

● **Table 7.1** Properties of types of tissue.

Furthermore, the data in the table explain why:

- ultrasound is almost completely reflected at an air–tissue boundary;
- a large amount is reflected at a bone–tissue boundary;
- very little is reflected at a muscle–tissue boundary.

So, if there is air between the transducer and the skin, the ratio I_r/I_0 is 0.99. This means that 99% of the incident energy is reflected at the skin and thus very little ultrasound will enter the body. The transducer must therefore be 'coupled' to the skin by a gel whose acoustic impedance is similar to that of the skin.

Likewise, using ultrasound little can be seen beyond the lungs or any other gas-filled cavities; the bladder must be full during examination and gas in the intestines avoided by careful positioning of the transducer. Also, nothing can be seen beyond bone, and reflections within bone will create difficulties in interpreting the image. This means that appropriate positioning is required to view the heart (through a gap between the ribs), and detailed examination of the adult brain is not possible.

Effect of frequency

The **resolution**, that is the detail that can be seen, improves with increasing frequency of the ultrasound, so it might be thought that the clearest pictures would be seen when the highest possible frequency (and therefore the lowest wavelength) is used. However, the amount of energy that is transferred as heat as the wave passes through tissue also increases as frequency increases; therefore a compromise must be made. At the optimum frequency, the beam will reach the organ being investigated in no more than 200 wavelengths.

SAQ 7.1

Use the data in *table 7.1* to calculate the ratio of ultrasound intensities I_r/I_0 for muscle to soft tissue and explain the significance of the result.

Ultrasound scanning

There are several different types of ultrasound scan that can be used, depending on the particular organ to be studied. These are the **A scan**, the **B scan** and the **Doppler scan**.

A scan

This is the simplest type of scan and is still used in some situations. A **pulse generator** is connected to the ultrasound transducer and the **time base of an** oscilloscope. The time base is connected to the x plates of the oscilloscope. The output of the receiver in the transducer is amplified and connected to the y plates of the oscilloscope. At the start of each sweep the pulse generator sends a pulse to the oscilloscope and, at the same time, triggers the transducer to send an ultrasound pulse into the tissue. When the ultrasound pulse hits a boundary between two different tissue types, some of the signal is reflected back to the receiver, where it is amplified and shown as a peak on the oscilloscope screen. The distance between the origin and the peak on the x axis will be proportional to the time taken for the ultrasound pulse to travel to the tissue boundary and back.

The amplitude of the received pulse will depend on the attenuation of the signal in the materials through which it has passed and on the acoustic impedance of any boundaries through which it has passed. The presence of attenuation means that the signals received from two interfaces

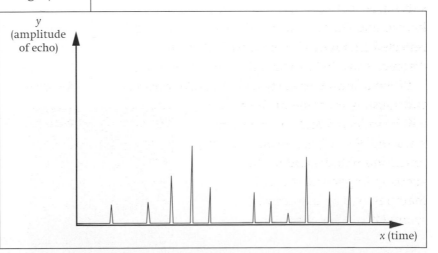

● **Figure 7.4** An A scan. The time between pairs of echoes gives the distance between the corresponding interfaces. Because of noise, the signal does not quite return to the axis between peaks.

between the same pair of materials at different depths will be different. In imaging, however, we require the signal from a given interface to be the same irrespective of position. In order to achieve this, signals from deeper in the body are amplified progressively, a process known as **swept gain**.

An **A scan** is thus a sequence of individual echoes due to reflections along one direction only. This is shown in *figure 7.4*. This type of scan is used, for example, to determine the thickness of the eye lens.

B scan

To obtain an image, the **B scanner** uses sensors attached to an ultrasonic transducer probe; these sensors define the position and orientation of the probe (and therefore of the beam) in a two-dimensional plane. For each situation of the probe, an A scan is obtained. A dot is then placed on the screen of a storage oscilloscope; this dot represents the calculated position of the reflecting surface. The intensity of the dot is dependent on the amplitude of the echo pulse. The ultrasound beam is 'swept' across the plane. The B scan image (*figure 7.5*) is built up from the superimposition of a collection of A scans. Since this takes several seconds, any movements within the organ will degrade the quality of the image. For example, it would be difficult to examine a pulsating heart with this method. This can be overcome using 'real-time' scanners, which are of two types – phased-array scanners and sector scanners.

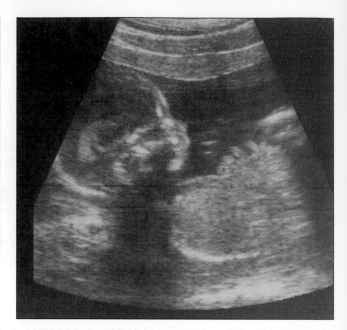

● **Figure 7.6** A foetus imaged by a real-time scanner; this is still one of the most common medical uses of ultrasound.

Real-time scanners

The **phased-array scanner** has several small transducers that are triggered individually very close together, with a small phase difference between each. This produces a composite ultrasound scan that does not need sensors to define the orientation of the beam. The arc covered by the beam from the transducers can be up to 90°.

Sector scanners use one or more transducers that are scanned mechanically across an arc of some 60°. In the single-transducer design, the transducer is rocked back and forth; this puts a high degree of mechanical strain on the components, however. More commonly, four transducers are mounted at 90° intervals on a rotating wheel. This is a simpler arrangement mechanically, but it requires careful matching of the transducers to obtain the same performance from each.

Both phased-array and sector scanners are small hand-held probes and they scan fast enough (25 images per second) for the images to be viewed as a 'film' on a television screen. The greatest use of these types of scan is during pregnancy, to check on the progress of

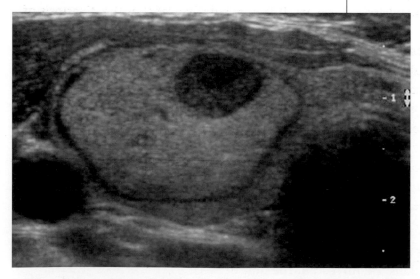

● **Figure 7.5** An ultrasonic B scan, showing an abnormal thyroid gland.

the foetus (*figure 7.6*). Measurements of the size of the foetus can be made and problems diagnosed at an early stage.

SAQ 7.2
Why is an ultrasound B scan used to examine a foetus rather than X-rays?

Doppler ultrasonography

Ultrasound can be used in a completely different way to measure movement. When an object that emits or reflects waves is moving, a stationary observer will find that the frequency of the waves received is different depending on whether the object is moving towards or away from the observer. This is known as the **Doppler effect**. Doppler ultrasound devices measure the frequency shift in the ultrasound signal reflected from a moving object, the frequency shift being proportional to the velocity of the object along the axis of the beam. This effect can be used to study the rate of blood flow in veins and arteries, where the moving objects are red blood cells.

There are two types of Doppler system, continuous and pulsed.

- In the **continuous Doppler** system, a narrow beam of waves, of between 2 and 10 MHz, is transmitted by one transducer while a second transducer acts as a receiver. The Doppler signals are generated by mixing the transmitted and received signals.
- A **pulsed Doppler** system gives range resolution, i.e. it defines a small volume at a given depth, the signal from which will be analysed. Range resolution is achieved by transmitting pulses of ultrasound and opening a receiver gate for a short period between pulses; the gate delay determines the maximum distance between the transducer and the reflecting surface. By using a large number of gates, blood flow can be examined all along the beam. By scanning in a similar way to the B scan, a two-dimensional image of the velocity pattern can be obtained.

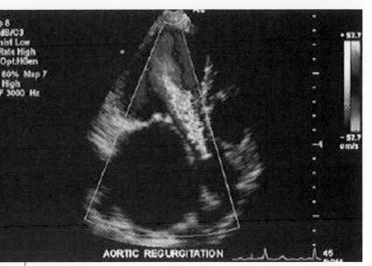

● **Figure 7.7** A flow ultrasound image.

Colour Doppler imaging

The technique of colour Doppler, or flow, imaging provides information about an event as it happens (i.e. in real time). The Doppler shift at each point of the scan is colour coded and superimposed on the normal two-dimensional grey-scale pictures that display anatomical information from a B scan. The colours red, blue, yellow, cyan and white are used to indicate the direction and speed of flow: red indicates a positive flow (i.e. the blood is travelling towards the transducer) and blue indicates a negative flow (away from the transducer). Different shades of blue and red represent different speeds. This technique is very important in cardiac studies, where it can be used to study abnormalities of blood flow within a damaged heart. It is particularly useful in the diagnosis of defects in the heart valves (*figure 7.7*).

SAQ 7.3
a Describe the Doppler effect and its use in ultra-sonography.
b Give an example of the medical use of this technique.

Other aspects

The main effect of the absorption of ultrasound in tissue is heating. At much higher intensities, a phenomenon called **cavitation** may occur. The rapid fluctuations in pressure caused by the passage of the ultrasound wave can cause dissolved gases (e.g. O_2 and CO_2 in blood) to form microbubbles; if the continuing changes in pressure cause these to collapse, tissues can be damaged both physically and chemically. At the powers used for diagnosis, there is no evidence of any harmful effects, although it is good practice to limit the exposure time, particularly for Doppler examinations.

Very high power ultrasound can be used for therapy. In physiotherapy departments, ultrasound is used to heat injured muscle, causing increased blood flow in order to accelerate the rate of healing. Another use is in a device known as a **lithotripter**; this uses ultrasound to break up kidney stones. Very high power ultrasound beams from two or more transducers are sent into the patient through gauze pads impregnated with coupling jelly. The patient is positioned so that the beams focus at the position of the kidney stone. The resulting high ultrasound intensity generated at this focus creates shock waves that shatter the stone into small fragments. These can then be passed out in the urine, avoiding the need for a major surgical operation.

SUMMARY

◆ Ultrasound waves are sound waves of frequencies above 20 000 Hz and are generated by the piezoelectric effect. This occurs when an alternating potential difference at the resonant frequency is placed across a piezoelectric crystal; this makes it alternately expand and contract.

◆ When an ultrasound pulse is transmitted through tissue, some of it is reflected and some transmitted through the various organs. The basic technique uses the equation $s = vt$ to calculate the position of a reflecting boundary.

◆ Acoustic impedance is defined as $Z = \rho v$, where ρ is the density of the substance and v is the speed of sound in the substance. The difference in Z-values across a boundary gives a measure of the energy reflected by the boundary.

◆ When the boundary is air to tissue, very little ultrasound is transmitted. This problem can be solved at the transducer–skin interface by using a gel to act as a coupling medium and so reduce the difference in impedance.

◆ An A scan produces echoes along one line, whereas a B scan combines A scans to build up information in two dimensions.

◆ Doppler scans image moving objects such as red blood cells.

◆ The main advantage of using ultrasound in examining soft tissue is that it has no side effects, unlike ionising radiations.

◆ Ultrasound has therapeutic as well as diagnostic uses, for example in treating sports injuries and kidney stones.

Questions

1   Ultrasound is a major imaging method. Why and when is it used rather than X-rays? Describe the key principles. Are there any disadvantages?

2   A relative is to receive an ultrasound scan and asks you to explain the use of the coupling medium, such as gel, that is placed on her body. She wants an explanation in terms of basic physics. Include in your answer the term acoustic impedance.

Magnetic resonance imaging

By the end of this chapter you should be able to:

1 understand the principles of *magnetic resonance imaging*;

2 understand the meaning of the terms *precession of nuclei*, *Larmor frequency*, *resonance* and *relaxation time*;

3 describe how MRI is used to obtain diagnostic information about internal structures in the body;

4 compare and contrast the advantages of using X-rays, ultrasound and MRI in obtaining information about body structures.

The technique of nuclear magnetic resonance (NMR) was developed in 1946 as a method of studying atomic and molecular structure, but it was not until 1973 that it was suggested that **magnetic resonance imaging** (MRI) might be useful in medicine.

Principle of nuclear magnetic resonance

The principle behind NMR is that the nuclei in certain atoms and molecules behave as small magnets, owing to their **spin**. Both protons and neutrons in the nucleus have spin, and it may be in one of two directions. If there are even numbers of both protons and neutrons then there are equal numbers spinning in each direction and so the effects cancel – we say that there is *no net spin*. However, if there is an odd number of either protons or neutrons then the spins cannot cancel. Nuclei that possess this net spin include hydrogen, phosphorus and carbon-13. The most important of these is hydrogen, which has only one proton and no neutrons and is common in the body (particularly as a constituent of water). Nuclei with a net spin have a magnetic 'north–south' axis, corresponding to their spin axis.

Normally the magnetic properties of hydrogen atoms are not detectable, since the magnetic axes of the nuclei are randomly aligned and the net effect is zero in all directions (*figure 8.1a*). If a strong magnetic field is applied, however, these nuclei will align themselves with it. Unlike compass needles, which would all point in the same direction, the magnetic nuclei will align themselves either in the same direction as the field or in exactly the opposite direction (*figure 8.1b*).

There is a very small preference for the same direction as the external field because the nuclei have slightly less energy in this position than if they point in the opposite direction. In a million nuclei, about seven more will point in the direction of the field than will oppose it. The net magnetic field due to nuclear spin is thus very weak.

Precession in external magnetic field

This very small nuclear magnetism in the presence of an external field would be impossible to detect if a nucleus remained pointing in exactly the same direction all the time. However, the direction of the magnetic axis of a nucleus in fact rotates around the direction of the external field, just as the axis of a spinning top rotates; this is called **precession** (*figure 8.1c*). The frequency of precession, the **Larmor frequency** ω_0, depends

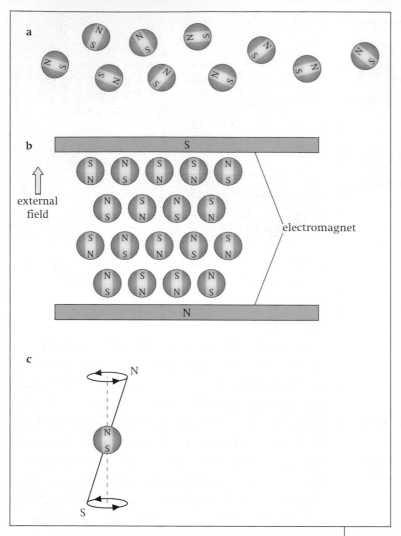

electromagnetic radiation at the Larmor frequency. Because each RF pulse has the same frequency as the precession of the nuclei, energy is transferred to the nuclei (a process known as **resonance**), which causes some of them to 'flip' from the lower-energy to the higher-energy alignment; these nuclei again precess in phase. After an RF pulse ends, the nuclei return to their original state (they are said to **relax**) by two electromagnetic processes.

In the first process, the energy is transferred directly to the surroundings of the nucleus, the lattice structure; this is called spin–lattice relaxation. The other process involves interactions between different spins and is called spin–spin relaxation. As they relax, the nuclei emit an RF signal, which is detected by a coil. The total emitted RF signal has an amplitude which is proportional to the number of nuclei present and which decreases over time. The graph of amplitude against time can be analysed to give two **relaxation times**, T_1 (for spin–lattice relaxation) and T_2 (for spin–spin relaxation). T_1 is between 2–10 times longer than T_2.

● **Figure 8.1** Diagrams representing the orientation of the magnetic axes of nuclei before and after application of a strong external magnetic field. **a** Random alignment; **b** when the field is applied the nuclei are forced to align either in the same direction or in the opposite direction to the field.   **c** The magnetic axis of each nucleus precesses, just like a spinning top.

upon the composition of the nucleus and the strength B_0 of the external magnetic field:

$$\omega_0 = \gamma B_0$$

where γ is the **gyromagnetic ratio** and relates the magnetism of a particle to its spin (its value for protons is approximately $42.5\,\text{MHz}\,\text{T}^{-1}$). The Larmor frequency lies in the radio frequency (RF) part of the electromagnetic spectrum.

Application of RF pulses

The precessing nuclei aligned in the external magnetic field are subjected to short pulses of RF

Magnetic resonance imaging (MRI)

Now we turn to the medical uses of magnetic resonance.

Hydrogen bound in the water in tissue has long relaxation times T_1 and T_2, whereas hydrogen bound in fat has short relaxation times. Therefore different tissues can be differentiated by their T_1 or T_2 values. For example, cerebrospinal fluid (largely water) has a long T_1 (several seconds), whereas white matter in the brain contains very little water and so has a short T_1 (several hundred milliseconds). Tumours tend to contain more water than normal tissue and so have an intermediate T_1 value. In terms of T_2, water has a value of around 3 seconds while white matter has a value of about 100 ms; tumours again have intermediate values.

SAQ 8.1

a Why do hydrogen nuclei exhibit magnetic resonance?

b What external fields must be applied for them to do this?

c What type of quantity can be deduced from a resonance experiment?

d How can normal and cancerous tissue be distinguished using this technique?

Apparatus for MRI

The apparatus used for MRI is shown in *figure 8.2*. There are five main features.

- A large electromagnet produces a high static magnetic field. The field strength is typically 0.5–2.0 tesla; for comparison, the Earth's magnetic field is 0.000 03–0.000 07 tesla. Superconducting magnets, which operate with the conducting coils kept at a temperature of −269°C (4 K), are used.

- A set of gradient coils produces a magnetic field that varies slightly with position.

- An RF coil transmits the RF pulse into the body.

- An RF receiver coil detects the signal emitted by the nuclei as they relax to their original orientation. This may be the same coil as the transmitter coil. In some cases, localised receiver coils are employed to obtain a larger signal as the nuclei relax. The most common of these is the head coil (*figure 8.3*).

- A computer controls the gradient coils and RF pulses and stores and analyses the received signals. It also reconstructs the data into **images** and displays them.

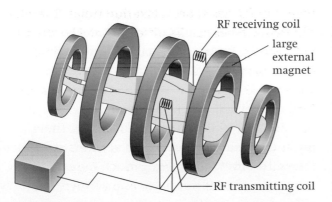

● **Figure 8.2** Apparatus used in magnetic resonance imaging (MRI).

RF receiving coil

large external magnet

RF transmitting coil

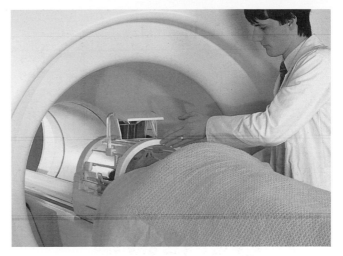

● **Figure 8.3** A head coil. This is placed around the patient's head and so gives a stronger signal.

Procedure

The patient is placed in the bore of the electro-magnet, which is typically 1.6 m long and has an internal diameter of 0.6 m for the central imaging section, which is 0.9 m long. The magnetic field is very uniform across the body, varying by less than 50 parts per million. The gradient coils then apply gradient fields, which are superimposed upon the static field to produce an effective magnetic field that is very slightly different at each point within the image volume. This means that the Larmor frequency will also vary slightly and so the signal from each point can be identified. The appropriate frequency RF pulse is then applied to flip the axes of the nuclei and the amplitude of relaxation signal is measured. An image, which is a map of the amplitude, is shown in *figure 8.4*.

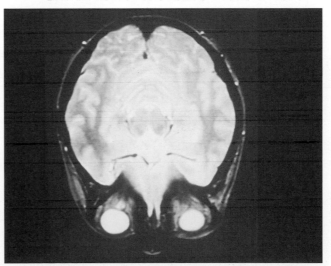

● **Figure 8.4** An MRI of the brain.

Data can also be collected after introducing paramagnetic substances into the body, in a manner similar to the use of X-ray contrast agents. These have small local magnetic fields that cause a shortening of the relaxation times and alter the signal amplitude from the target area to produce greater image contrast.

The MR signal is affected by spinning nuclei that are moving and this can be used to produce an image of flowing blood, as shown in *figure 8.5*. This is known as MR angiography. It is possible also to obtain images of parts of the brain that are involved in certain tasks. For example, if a patient is shown a flashing light pattern, then the part of the brain associated with visual processing will be stimulated and local blood flow will increase. By

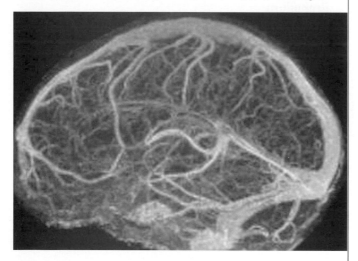

● **Figure 8.5** An angiogram produced by MRI.

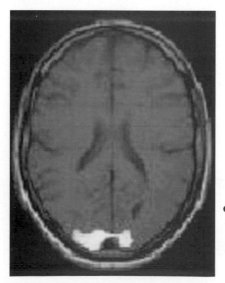

● **Figure 8.6** In functional MRI, images are obtained by subtraction.

taking an image before stimulation and subtracting it from one taken during stimulation, an image demonstrating changes (i.e. only the stimulated area) will be obtained; this is known as **functional** MRI (fMRI) (*figure 8.6*).

Advantages and disadvantages of MRI

There are several advantages in using MRI.

■ The most important advantage is that the method does not use ionising radiation which, even in small doses, creates a radiation hazard to both the patient and the staff.

■ MRI gives better soft-tissue contrast than computed X-ray tomography and generates data from a three-dimensional volume simultaneously.

■ The information in the computer can be displayed on a screen as a slice or section in any direction or as a simulated three-dimensional image.

■ There are no moving mechanisms involved in MRI; it just uses changing currents and magnetic fields.

■ There is no sensation, after-effect or side-effect at the field strengths used for routine diagnostic imaging. A relaxed patient can even sleep during the examination, although there is noise generated from the switching of the gradient coils.

There are some disadvantages in using MRI. For example, metallic objects such as surgical pins or clips can become heated, and cardiac pacemakers can be upset since most are designed to be controlled by applying magnetic or radio fields; patients with either of these cannot be imaged in this way. One hazard is that loose steel objects could be drawn into the magnet. The room must also be screened from external radio fields.

MRI, ultrasound and X-rays

MRI and ultrasound share the fact that they do not use ionising radiation and are thus safer than X-rays. However, MRI gives a much higher spatial resolution than ultrasound, as do X-rays. The X-ray CT scanner is better than MRI for visualising bony structures. Ultrasound can give real-time images of, for example, the beating heart – this is only just becoming possible with MRI. Claustrophobia is a problem with around 3%–5% of patients with MRI. The development of short-bore 'open' systems is addressing this.

SUMMARY

◆ The nuclei of certain atoms behave like magnets and become aligned either in the same or opposite direction by an external magnetic field.

◆ The magnetic axis of the nucleus precesses around the direction of the external magnetic field.

◆ The frequency of precession is called the Larmor frequency and is dependent on the composition of the nucleus and on the magnetic field.

◆ When an RF pulse has the same frequency as the Larmor frequency of the nuclei, resonance occurs, and some spins flip.

◆ The relaxation time is the time taken for the nuclei to return to their original state after the pulse is applied.

◆ MRI is used primarily to examine structures containing hydrogen, which produce images that differ depending on whether the hydrogen is surrounded by water or fat.

◆ MRI has considerable advantages over other methods; for example, it is particularly useful for locating soft-tissue tumours.

Question

Magnetic resonance imaging has been described as a major advance in the safe imaging of the human body.

a What are the key features of the physical process?

b Describe the key parts of the machine that allow such images to be obtained.

c Why is it a safe method?

CHAPTER 9

Radiotherapy

By the end of this chapter you should be able to:

1 describe the action of *ionising radiation* in the treatment of malignancies;

2 describe how a *treatment plan* is prepared;

3 describe how X-rays, γ-rays and radioactive sources are used in various types of therapy.

Radiotherapy is a branch of medical treatment that uses ionising radiation as a medicine. The main use of radiotherapy is to kill off cancerous cells while sparing normal tissue. During treatment the affected parts of the body might be given large radiation doses, divided into smaller, regular amounts and delivered over a period of several weeks. The treatment may use external beams of radiation (usually X-rays but also electrons) or the implantation of radioactive sources or the administration of unsealed radionuclides.

Action of radiation in therapy

During the treatment of malignancies, both when using X-rays and radioactive sources, it is important that the cancerous cells are killed and that any damage to normal tissue is strictly limited. Rather than give a single large dose of radiation, the radiation is split into a number of small doses called **fractions**, which are given over a period of time. This fractionation technique has two advantages.

■ Cells are more sensitive to the action of ionising radiation when they are dividing, but may spend more time in a state in which they are not dividing. Cells that happened not to be radiosensitive during one fraction may be radiosensitive during another and so be killed then. Cancerous cells divide more rapidly than normal cells and so are more likely to be radiosensitive during treatment.

■ Normal cells recover more rapidly between fractions than do cancer cells, and so a higher total

radiation dose can be tolerated by the patient than if a single, larger, dose were given.

It is useful to define the term **target volume**, which is the volume of tissue within the patient that is to be irradiated to a given absorbed dose in a certain time. The energy given to the target volume must be significantly higher than that given to the surrounding healthy tissue if dangerous side-effects are to be avoided. This is particularly important if the surrounding areas include radiosensitive tissues and organs such as the spinal cord, kidneys and the lens of the eye.

Treatment planning

To achieve the best results, the required distribution of the radiation, called the **dose distribution**, must be calculated accurately.

First, the doctor needs information about the position and the exact extent of the tumour. This is obtained from X-ray, CT or MRI images of the target volume from different angles; MRI scanners are particularly useful for soft-tissue tumours. Digital images are transferred directly to the treatment planning computer via a local area network. The doctor then specifies the required radiation dose to the tumour and the physicist establishes the best geometric combination of beam directions to give a cell-killing radiation dose to the target while minimising the radiation dose to surrounding normal tissue, i.e. a satisfactory dose distribution.

In order to do this, the treatment planning computer requires data on the radiation beam

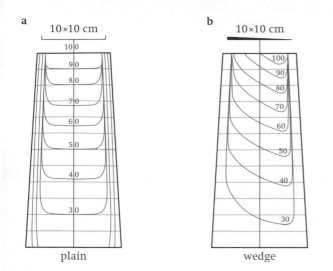

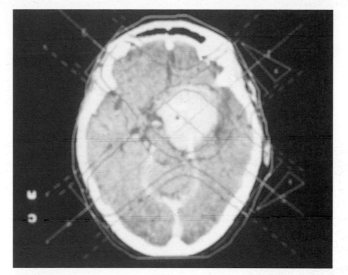

● **Figure 9.1** Isodose curves of a linear accelerator, as measured in a water tank. The beam enters the water from above. The number labelling a curve represents the percentage of the surface dose received. **a** Unmodified; **b** modified by a thin lead wedge placed above the surface of the tank.

produced by the treatment machine. This is in the form of a set of **isodose curves** joining points of equal radiation dose, measured in a water tank, which simulates a typical patient. In *figure 9.1a*, the isodose curves for an unmodified beam are shown.

Now the output of the treatment machine has to be 'customised' to the patient in question. The basic isodose curves of the treatment machine were produced under the assumption that body tissue is homogeneous and has the same attenuation properties as water. However, the presence of tissues with different properties, particularly air cavities such as the lungs, can greatly alter the isodose curves. The shape of the body surface will also make the isodose curves asymmetric.

Therefore, in each direction of use the treatment beam is modified by thin lead wedges (*figure 9.1b*). These wedges also compensate for body curvature, 'trim' the beam near a critical organ, or ensure dose uniformity within the target volume when the beam directions are not spaced equally around the patient.

The treatment planning computer then works out the total dose distribution that will result from irradiating the patient from the various different angles. This is done by superimposing the isodose curves and summing to get the total dose

● **Figure 9.2** Treatment plan for a brain tumour; in this case, four beam angles will be used, aligned so that the tumour is the only tissue that will be irradiated on all four occasions.

at each point. The dose delivered from each angle may be different. Several treatment schedules will be calculated and the best one, which gives the correct dose distribution, will be selected for use. A final treatment plan is shown in *figure 9.2* for a patient suffering from carcinoma of the brain.

Use of a simulator

In order to check the accuracy of the treatment plan prior to treatment, the patient will be examined in a simulator. This machine has a rotating gantry similar to the treatment machine, but instead is fitted with a diagnostic X-ray system and an image intensifier. The system produces a film of the area to be treated, with markers showing the edges of the treatment field as calculated in the treatment plan. These test X-ray images are obtained to check that the target volume will be irradiated as planned.

SAQ 9.1
Why is a dose treatment plan needed and what is meant by isodose curves?

External beam therapy

The normal radiation source used in external beam therapy is a **linear accelerator**, which produces X-rays by accelerating electrons to a high

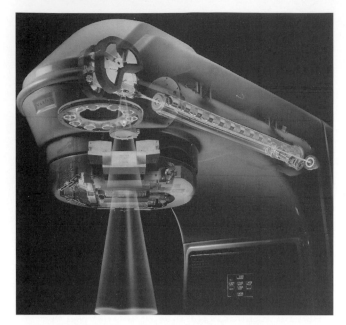

● **Figure 9.3** Schematic diagram of a linear accelerator used in external beam therapy.

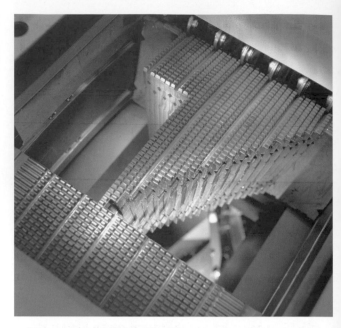

● **Figure 9.4** Multi-leaf collimator for a linear accelerator.

velocity using a radio frequency wave. The high-energy electron beam is deflected by a magnet and focussed onto a target in which the X-rays are produced (*figure 9.3*). The conversion to X-rays is more efficient at large energies (4–20 MeV) than at the voltages used for ordinary diagnostic X-rays. At these energies, there is very little absorption in the body caused by the photoelectric effect (see page 38) and so attenuation by different tissues is quite similar.

The X-ray beam is trimmed to the desired shape by moveable shutters in a collimator. Conventional collimators give rise to a rectangular beam. The dimensions are chosen to ensure that all the target volume is enclosed within the beam, but this means that some normal tissue is irradiated also. Multi-leaf collimators have been introduced, which comprise up to 120 pairs of lead fingers. These can be moved independently, so that complex beam shapes can be selected (*figure 9.4*). The beam itself can thus be tailored to the exact shape of the tumour at each beam angle, minimising the radiation dose to normal tissue.

The positioning of the beam can be checked prior to treatment by using a light source arranged to simulate the beam exactly. The whole accelerator, target and collimator is mounted to rotate about the treatment couch, which can move in all three dimensions (*figure 9.5*). Usually, the tumour is at some distance below the skin. It can be seen from

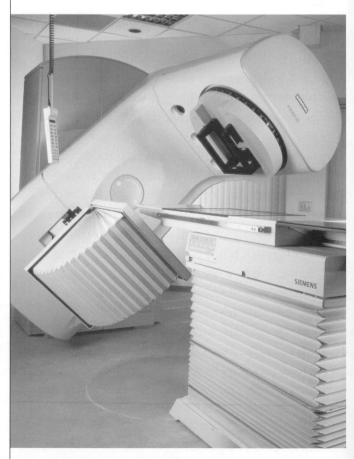

● **Figure 9.5** Linear accelerator. The treatment head is at the upper right. The device at lower left, opposite the treatment head, is an imaging system that takes low-resolution images of X-rays transmitted through a patient in order to check the accuracy of the beam position.

figures 9.1 and 9.2 that if the irradiation were carried out from one direction only the overlying normal tissue would receive a higher radiation dose than the tumour. In order to avoid this, as mentioned earlier, treatment is carried out from a number of different angles. The patient is positioned so that the tumour is at the centre of rotation of the accelerator; in this way, the tumour is irradiated from all angles, but normal tissues receive only a fraction of the total dose.

Gamma rays from a cobalt teletherapy unit can be used instead of X-rays, for some types of cancer. The radiation source is a pellet of cobalt-60. This emits high-energy gamma radiation with a half-life of 5.3 years. Unlike the linear accelerator, the radiation cannot be switched off, so the cobalt pellet has to be stored in a totally shielded position. It is moved mechanically from the storage position to the treatment position in a shielded sphere that has an aperture from which the treatment beam emerges. The edges of the treatment beam are less well defined than for the linear accelerator because of the relatively large size of the radioactive source. This makes it more difficult to achieve a sharp fall-off in radiation dose at the edges of the target volume and so these machines tend to be used where this problem is not so important, as in total body irradiation. Once again, the machine rotates about the patient from one treatment position to another.

In both X-ray and gamma ray treatment, it is vital that the patient is placed in exactly the same position for each fraction. The treatment field is marked on the patient's skin, sometimes by tattoo, and an alignment system that employs a low-power helium–neon laser is used.

SAQ 9.2

Many hospitals have replaced their cobalt sources with linear accelerators. Suggest why this change has been made.

If the target in the linear accelerator is moved out of the beam path, the electron beam itself can be used to treat tumours at shallow depths, for example certain skin tumours. Since the tumour is superficial, the electron beam is placed directly over the tumour.

There are problems with external beam therapy: for example, large volumes of tissue are irradiated, including tissue between the body surface and the tumour. Shielding by bone can also be a problem. Some of these problems can be overcome by using implant or radionuclide therapy, in which alpha or beta sources are deposited at the site of the tumour.

Alpha and beta emissions, together with low-energy X-rays and gamma rays, are classed as '**non-penetrating**' radiations. This means that they are wholly absorbed within the patient's body and so are not useful in diagnostic imaging, since they only increase the radiation dose to the patient without making it possible to produce an image. However, they can be useful in therapy.

Surface and implant therapy

Surface and implant therapy is also known as **sealed source therapy**.

Since the beginning of the twentieth century when Pierre and Marie Curie first prepared a sample of radium-226, small radioactive sources in many shapes and sizes have been used in radiotherapy. Metal tubes and needles packed with radium-226 or caesium-137 have been particularly popular, and in recent years, iridium-191 has been introduced. Plaques and shaped eye applicators containing cobalt-60, strontium-90 and ruthenium-106 are also available (figure 9.6).

● **Figure 9.6** Applicators for surface therapy.

The disadvantage of using this kind of therapy is that the dose patterns are very uneven. Underdoses of radiation can be avoided only by allowing some regions of overdose. However, these are small and are quite tolerable and repairable.

These kinds of sources can be used in three different ways.

■ **Surface applicators** are arrays of sources placed near to or in contact with the patient's skin for superficial treatments. They are used, for example, in treating the eye.

■ **Interstitial implants** use radioactive wire or arrays of needle-like radioactive sources implanted directly into the target volume. They can be used for breast cancer.

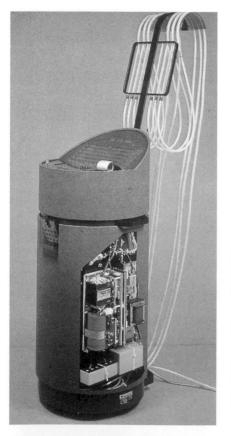

● **Figure 9.7** Afterloading device for use with implant therapy. The tubes for connection to the patient can be seen.

■ With **intracavitary methods**, the sources are sealed into special containers and inserted into the appropriate body cavity. These are frequently used for the treatment of cancer of the cervix. Interstitial and intracavitary treatments generally take a few days, during which the sources remain in the patient. It is now possible to use high dose rate 'after-loading' techniques, which significantly reduce treatment times. These methods involve the insertion of tubes, or hollow applicators attached to tubes, into the organ or tissues to be treated. During this operation no radioactive sources are present. After the tubes are correctly positioned they are connected to the source storage device and the sources are blown into position using compressed air (*figure 9.7*). This occurs after the patient has been transferred to a specially protected room. With some of these treatments, the final distribution of radioactive sources in the patient may not be exactly the same as the planned, idealised distribution and radiographic checks are necessary.

Unsealed source therapy

In **unsealed source therapy**, the radionuclide is carried through the body by means of a pharmaceutical. The complex is called a **radiopharmaceutical**; see also chapter 6.

This kind of radiotherapy, known as **targeting**, can only be used in those cases in which a pharmaceutical exists that can be used to carry the radionuclide to the site of the tumour. The radiopharmaceutical is usually in liquid form and is administered orally or by intravenous injection. In some cases, a capsule containing the radiopharmaceutical is swallowed.

Use of radioactive iodine, ^{131}I

A common example of this kind of radiotherapy is the treatment of an overactive thyroid (known as thyrotoxicosis), which was first used in 1948. The thyroid gland requires iodine to produce the hormone thyroxine. Iodine is only found in minute amounts in the rest of the body, so radioactive iodine introduced into the body will mostly collect in the thyroid. The radioactive iodine is used in either liquid or capsule form.

The amount of radioactive iodine, ^{131}I, to be administered is usually based on a simple calculation according to the size of the gland and the level of overactivity. There are certain restrictions that patients must observe because of the risk of irradiating other people. For example, journeys on public transport should be limited to one hour and patients should stay at home until the radioactivity has dropped to a safe level.

Higher amounts of ^{131}I may be administered to destroy a thyroid cancer. In this case, the patient must stay in hospital for a few days until the safe level is reached.

SAQ 9.3

In radiotherapy, sometimes radioactive sources are placed inside the body. Explain why this method of treatment will not always be satisfactory.

Question

Outline the preparation of a treatment plan. Describe typical cases that may be treated by external beam therapy, sealed source therapy or unsealed source therapy.

SUMMARY

◆ Radiation is given in a number of small doses (fractions) to increase the chance of irradiating cells that are dividing; at this time they are most sensitive to radiation. Also, the rate of repair of cancer cells is slower than normal cells, so cancer cells are likely to be killed by several small doses whereas normal cells recover.

◆ Treatment planning determines how the required dose distribution can be achieved. The isodose curves of the treatment machine are modified with lead wedges for each beam direction, to suit each particular case.

◆ X-rays or other ionising radiations provide the main sources used in treatment.

◆ In external beam therapy, by rotating the source the cancerous cells always receive the radiation but the healthy cells only receive a small amount of radiation.

◆ In surface or implant therapy, sealed radionuclides are placed in the body. Sometimes 'after-loading' techniques are used.

◆ In unsealed source therapy, a pharmaceutical conveys the radionuclide to the required site in the body.

CHAPTER 10

Light in diagnosis and therapy

By the end of this chapter you should be able to:

1 explain the structure of optical fibres and their use in endoscopes, including the importance of *coherent* bundles of fibres, *resolution* and *brightness* of the image;

2 describe examples of the uses of *endoscopes*;

3 describe the use of *lasers* in medicine, including as a scalpel and as a coagulator;

4 understand that laser surgery has advantages compared to conventional surgery;

5 describe what is meant by *photochemotherapy*.

The visible and near-visible (infrared to ultraviolet) portions of the electromagnetic spectrum are used in medicine for both diagnosis and therapy.

Endoscopes

Endoscopes use fibre optics (see *Physics 1*, page 157) to send a light along a tube and return an image so that it is possible to view inside the body. Endoscopes can be used along the tubes of the body, e.g. (1) along the trachea into the lungs, (2) along the oesophagus into the stomach and intestines, and (3) into the bladder and bowels. They can also be inserted through a small incision or 'key-hole' in order to view internal parts of the body without the need for major surgery (so-called **key-hole surgery**). A key feature is that an endoscope is a cold light source, so there is no heat delivered inside the body.

Two different arrangements of fibre bundles are used. If the fibres have exactly the same relative positions at each end of a bundle then an image can be **resolved** at the other end of the bundle from the object; this is a **coherent** bundle. If the fibres are arranged in a random way then the bundle is **incoherent**. Incoherent fibre bundles are cheaper to produce. In both cases, the ends of the bundle are evenly cut and polished. The brightness of the light received back is the same for coherent and incoherent bundles.

An endoscope is shown in *figure 10.1* and consists of four parts:

■ an incoherent bundle, which is used to send light down the tube;

■ a coherent return bundle, which has a lens at the bottom end and is used to send reflected light back up the tube so that an image can be formed;

■ a channel for the water which is used to clean the lens;

■ another channel that allows liquids to be taken out of the body or biopsy probes to be put into the body to obtain very small tissue samples.

The tube is round and reasonably flexible. A portion at the far end is more flexible and can be moved around by the operator by means of control wires.

Almost all wavelengths of light can be passed along an endoscope except those that are in the infrared region; the quartz in the fibres absorbs some of these wavelengths.

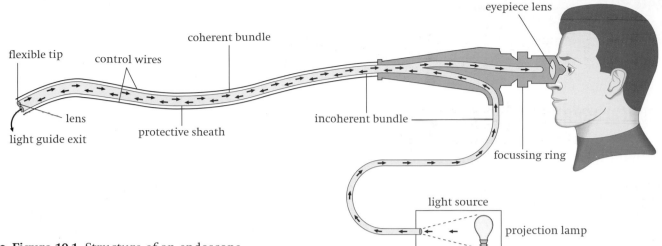

● **Figure 10.1** Structure of an endoscope.

a What are the advantages in using an endoscope to see inside the body?

b Explain how different types of fibre bundle are used in the endoscope.

Lasers

The word 'laser' is an acronym for **l**ight **a**mplification by **s**timulated **e**mission of **r**adiation. This is a resonance phenomenon whereby a previously excited atom, when struck by a photon of the correct wavelength, emits *two* photons at this wavelength and in the same direction. Thus, by repeated multiplication of photons an intense beam is rapidly built up. Lasers have two particular features that make them useful in medical treatments.

■ The radiation produced is all of the same wavelength. In contrast, an ordinary white light source, even when passed through a coloured filter, will still contain a mixture of wavelengths.

■ The light over the whole cross-section of the exit beam is in phase and can be focussed to a spot, achieving very high power densities in comparison to a normal light source.

It is the power density, rather than the total power, that allows the beam to cut through materials. The output of a typical school helium–neon laser is perhaps 0.1 mW, with beam diameter typically 3 mm at a distance of 2 m. This gives a power density of 14 W m^{-2}. For comparison, a 100 W lamp at the same distance spreads its energy over a sphere of surface area $4\pi r^2$. As the lamp can be taken to be only 10% efficient in its conversion of electrical energy to light, this gives an intensity of 0.2 W m^{-2} at a distance of $r = 2$ m. The laser mentioned above, however, gives a power density 70 times greater. This means that particular care should be taken to avoid laser light entering the eye, even though the overall power output might seem very low.

The output from a laser can be pulsed or continuous, depending on the type of treatment to be given. *Table 10.1* gives the details of different lasers used in medicine. The data shown are for continuous power outputs unless otherwise stated.

Type of laser	Wavelength (nm)	Typical power
Excimer	193	20 W
Argon	488 or 514	0.5–1 W
Dye	550–700 (depending on dye)	100–500 mW
Helium–neon	633	1–5 mW
Gallium arsenide	910	1 mW
Neodymium yttrium aluminium garnet (YAG)	1064	25–50 W 50 kW (pulsed) 1 MW (Q-switched)
Carbon dioxide	10 600	20 W

● **Table 10.1** Properties of some types of laser. Q-switching is a technique that contains a laser until its power is greatly increased.

SAQ 10.2

Describe two features of a laser that make it useful in medical treatments.

General medical uses of lasers

Lasers are used in medical treatment in a variety of ways. Three common treatments are described below.

■ **Using the laser as a scalpel**

When surgeons cut through tissue with a scalpel they also cut through minor blood vessels. These bleed into the working area and make it more difficult to see the part of the body under treatment. A carbon dioxide laser, however, can be used to allow bloodless surgery. As the laser cuts through tissue, heat from the beam will cause the tissue (including the small blood vessels) to shrink and harden. Water in the tissue will be vaporised. There will be a very slight charring at the edges of the blood vessels but this is almost unnoticeable.

■ **Removal of birthmarks and tattoos**

A common birthmark is a port-wine-coloured stain on the skin, caused by the abnormal growth of blood vessels beneath the skin. An argon laser, which produces a blue–green light, can be used to reduce the mark. The light will be absorbed by the dark blood vessels and will seal them (*figure 10.2*). This usually leaves a slight scar. Certain tattoos can also be partially removed. In this case, the laser energy is absorbed by the dye molecules used in the tattoo, causing them to break up.

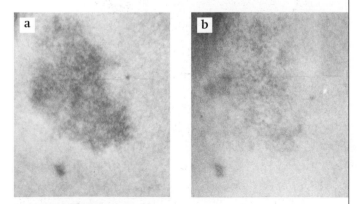

● **Figure 10.2** A birthmark **a** before laser treatment and **b** afterwards.

■ **Using a laser with an endoscope**

A neodymium YAG laser can be used with an endoscope to destroy cancers that block a patient's airway. The treatment will not cure the patient but will make them more comfortable. Recently this type of laser has been used also to vaporise blood clots and other deposits in veins and arteries. This has required the development of small-diameter, very flexible, fibre optics that can be threaded into the patient's blood vessels. At present, success has been obtained in treating blood clots in the leg. In the future, the technique may be extended to unblocking the arteries in the heart.

Laser treatment of eye problems

Lasers can be used to treat a variety of different eye problems.

■ **Detached retina**

Sometimes the retina can detach itself from the rear of the eyeball. It can be welded back into place using a pulsed ruby or argon laser. The laser is focussed on to a particular spot, melting the tissue and forming a weld. A series of welds is used to re-attach the retina completely.

■ **Diabetic retinopathy**

Some people who suffer from diabetes experience a progressive deterioration of their vision. This happens because a network of new and 'leaky' blood vessels gradually develops in the retina, from the edge inwards. Since blood is opaque, vision is lost. An argon laser can be used to seal the vessels: the dark blood vessels absorb the light and change it to heat, which causes sealing. The treated area of the retina is destroyed, but further proliferation of the blood vessels is prevented so that the rest of the patient's sight will not be affected (*figure 10.3*).

■ **Strands of tissue**

A **cataract** is a developing opacity of the lens (see page 15). This can be corrected by removing the natural lens and replacing it with a plastic lens. However, strands of opaque tissue can grow behind the new lens as the body's defence mechanisms recognise the new lens as a foreign body. A pulsed neodymium YAG laser can be used to split the strands of tissue without

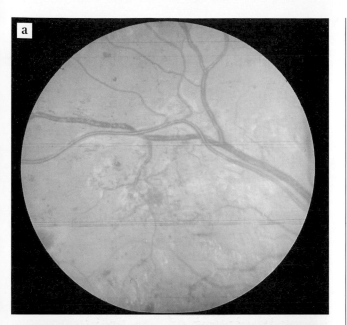

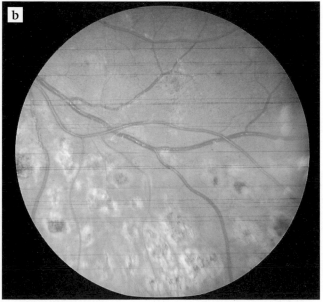

• **Figure 10.3** The retina **a** before laser treatment for diabetic retinopathy and **b** afterwards – the scars left by the laser can be seen. This treatment, at the edges of the retina, saves the central part.

damaging the lens. The correction to the patient's sight will be immediate.

SAQ 10.3 _____

The visible spectrum ranges from 400–700 nm.

a Using *table 10.1*, decide which lasers operate in the infrared region of the spectrum.

b A laser has a power output of 20 W. Calculate the time required to dissipate 150 J of energy.

Laser correction of eye defects

A relatively recent laser technique allows a permanent correction to the eye defects described in chapter 2. This technique uses an excimer laser either to produce incisions in the corneal surface, so that it can be slightly reshaped, or to reprofile the corneal surface by vaporising excess tissue. Care must be taken not to impair the transparency of the cornea.

In the correction of short sight (myopia), the laser light, which is transmitted in the ultraviolet region of the spectrum, is delivered through a set of apertures (*figure 10.4*). The apertures decrease in diameter round the wheel. Then, as the wheel is rotated from one aperture to the next, smaller one, more of the central area of the cornea is removed than the edge. The length of time that each of the apertures remains open is controlled by a computer. The treatment uses a series of lenses and control systems that allow the light to be correctly focussed on to the required part of the eye.

A different set of apertures is used in the correction of long sight. The purpose now is to remove more of the tissue at the edge of the cornea than at the centre. This is done by progressively larger openings which increase the curvature of the cornea. The aperture wheel is shown in *figure 10.5* (overleaf).

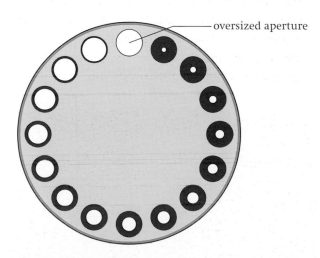

• **Figure 10.4** Aperture wheel used in the correction of short sight. The apertures let in more of the laser light through the centre than the edge of the treated area, so that more of the cornea is removed in the centre, decreasing the curvature.

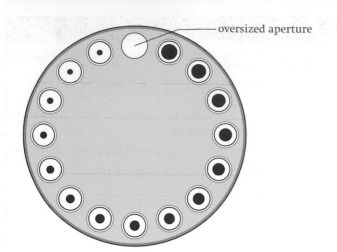

● **Figure 10.5** Aperture wheel used in the correction of long sight. The central disc in each aperture shields the centre of the cornea so that more is removed from the edges, increasing the curvature.

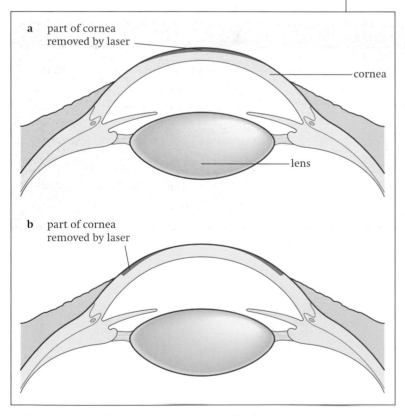

● **Figure 10.6** Effect on the cornea of laser treatment for the correction of **a** short sight and **b** long sight.

Figure 10.6 shows the effect on the cornea of correction for short and long sight.

Astigmatism may also be corrected, using a series of rectangles that can be aligned and then rotated.

Drawbacks

The application of the excimer laser for this type of treatment has only recently been developed. It is not successful in every case and has been found to create other defects or to produce scarring of tissue in some cases. About 10% of patients have reported problems after treatment.

Photochemotherapy

In addition to its uses in the correction of eye defects, ultraviolet (UV) light is also used in other medical treatments, particularly for the skin condition psoriasis. In this case, the portion of the UV spectrum from 320 to 380 nm, known as UVA, is used in conjunction with the drug psoralen. Psoralen is taken up preferentially by the diseased cells and is activated by exposure to UVA radiation. It combines with the DNA in the cell and inhibits cell replication. Normal skin cells do not take up psoralen and so are unaffected by the radiation except for a sunburn-like reddening. Before treatment is carried out, a quantity called the **minimum phototoxicity dose** (MPD) is first determined; this is the dose of UVA that just causes reddening of the skin. Then the patient swallows the drug; this is followed by irradiation about two hours later, the initial dose of UVA used being the MPD. Patients may be treated as often as daily until the condition is cleared, and the dose of radiation can be increased as required.

SUMMARY

- The endoscope involves two sets of fibre optics. An incoherent set sends down light to the area under investigation and a coherent set receives back a clear image.

- Endoscopes are used to examine the insides of the gastrointestinal tract, lungs and bladder and for keyhole surgery.

- Lasers can be used in the following ways: as scalpels; for removal of birthmarks; for palliative treatment in conjunction with an endoscope; for the treatment of detached retina; for other eye problems such as diabetic retinopathy and opaque tissue growth behind lens replacements.

- Laser treatment does not involve any conventional surgery such as cutting into tissue.

- Lasers can also be used to correct eye defects by reshaping the cornea, but there are problems in about 10% of cases.

- UV light is used in photochemotherapy.

Questions

1 Endoscopes are used to examine the inside of the body and are used as part of keyhole surgery. State the advantage of using endoscopes in examinations inside the body. In your answer describe the key parts of an endoscope.

2 An excimer laser is used in treatment for reducing the curvature of the cornea.
   a What are the key points about this technique?
   b The laser is used for a total time of 1 minute 30 seconds. Use information from *table 10.1* on page 75 to calculate the energy used.

Answers to questions

Chapter 1

Self-assessment questions

1.1 In order to push, your arms have to try to straighten; this requires the triceps to contract.

1.2 Clockwise moment = anticlockwise moment, so

$lT = l'M$

Since $T = mg = 98\,\text{N}$, $l = 0.35\,\text{m}$, $l' = 0.02\,\text{m}$ then

$$M = \frac{0.35 \times 98}{0.02}$$

$$= 1715\,\text{N}$$

1.3 Weight acting down $W = 75 \times 9.8 = 735\,\text{N}$.
Balancing moments,

$M \sin 10° = W \sin 70°$

so

$M = 3977\,\text{N}$

Thus

$S = M \cos 10° + W \cos 70° = 4168\,\text{N}$

End-of-chapter questions

1 Horizontally,

$M \cos 15° = R$

Vertically,

$M \sin 15° = W = 13\,\text{N}$

Thus $M = 50.2\,\text{N}$, $R = 48.5\,\text{N}$.

2 The spine is a rigid structure and should be kept vertical to avoid rupture to the discs. If the body is bent at an angle of 60° then the force of the pelvis acting on the spine is eight times the body weight. Figures similar to those in the chapter can be used to illustrate this idea.

Chapter 2

Self-assessment questions

2.1 a The cornea is the outer part of the eye and provides the main refraction of the light. The lens is an active element, which provides the fine adjustments.

b Without the face mask, there is not much bending of light rays coming into the eye since the refractive indices of water and of the cornea are not very different and so the eye cannot focus the rays. With the mask, the refractive index of the air trapped in the mask makes the focussing similar to that experienced above the water.

2.2 Focal length in metres $= \dfrac{1}{\text{power}}$

$$= \frac{1}{-0.25\,\text{D}}$$

$$= -4.0\,\text{m}$$

2.3 a The depth of field is the range of distances over which an object will be in focus.

b The eye can accommodate because the lens can change its power by contraction or relaxation of the ciliary muscles. This ability decreases with age because the lens becomes less flexible.

2.4 Using the lens formula

$$\frac{1}{u} + \frac{1}{v} = \frac{1}{f}$$

we require the value of $1/f$ that will give $u = \infty$ when $v = 0.02\,\text{m}$:

$$\frac{1}{0.02} + \frac{1}{\infty} = 50\,\text{D}$$

This is the total power required for the person's far point to be at infinity.
If their unaided far point is actually at $1.0\,\text{m}$ then the minimum power of the eye must be

$$\frac{1}{1.0} + \frac{1}{0.02} = 51\,\text{D}$$

Thus the power of the correcting lens required to take the person's far point to infinity is $-1\,\text{D}$.

2.5 a At the near point, the power of the eye is $1/2.0 + 1/0.02 = 50.5\,\text{D}$. To bring the near point to a distance of $0.25\,\text{m}$ needs a total power of $1/0.25 + 1/0.02 = 54\,\text{D}$. This means a spectacle lens of $+3.5\,\text{D}$ is required.

b If the accommodation is 3 D and the combined power of the eye and the correcting lens at the near point is 54 D then the combined power at the far point must be 51 D. Given that v is again 0.02 m and $1/f$ = 51 D then the far point must now be at a distance u of 1.0 m.

2.6 a Since the object changes shape with angle, the spectacle lens must have a cylindrical correction. This is used to compensate for uneven curvature of the cornea, i.e. astigmatism.

b Since a person with astigmatism focusses light in a vertical plane and light in a horizontal plane at different points, the power of the lens will need to be greater in one direction than in the perpendicular direction.

2.7 a The eye is most sensitive to this colour, which also lies in the middle of the visible wavelength range, and so the lenses are designed to reflect more light of this wavelength.

b Three types of cone contain pigments sensitive to different wavelength ranges of light. The molecules are broken down by the absorption of light, producing small electrical potentials. They then regenerate.

2.8 Red and green are the colours most often confused. Therefore difficulties may occur with wiring or signals. Electricians, train drivers, printers, car drivers may experience difficulties if they are colour blind.

2.9 The use of vertical visual edges lead the eye upwards and round. Visual edges emphasise the pattern of the vaulting. The subdued colour of the stonework gives an effect of rest. Where colours such as red and gold are used, it will be for the parts of the building on which attention has to be focussed.

End-of-chapter questions

1 a The key features of the eye are the cornea, aqueous humour, iris, lens, vitreous humour, retina and optic nerve. Their functions are detailed at the beginning of this chapter. The cornea does the bulk of the refraction in the eye but the lens provides the fine adjustments.

b Using

$$\frac{1}{u} + \frac{1}{v} = \frac{1}{f}$$

first set u = 150 cm = 1.5 m and v = 0.02 m. This gives the power of the eye lens at maximum

accommodation as 1/1.5 + 1/0.02 = 50.7 D. The required total power is found by putting u = 0.25 m and v = 0.02 m: we obtain 1/0.25 + 1/0.02 = 54 D. Thus a lens of power +3.3 D is needed.

2 Admissions area: bright and light colours. There is a need to create an illusion of space and to encourage a business-like atmosphere, so that people move quickly through this area. Notices should be in bold lettering and easily seen; therefore suitable colours, with good contrast, are needed for text and background.

Waiting area: colours that will create warmth and a calming effect. For example, the walls could be pale green and the floor a soft reddish-brown colour, to shrink the floor space and so produce a cosier feeling.

Play area: bold colours to create a busy effect and movement but part of the area in pastel colours to help create a quieter atmosphere for reading etc.

Chapter 3

Self-assessment questions

3.1 The pinna is used to collect and direct the sound down the auditory canal. The diaphragm at the inner end of the canal, i.e. the eardrum, vibrates when the sound reaches it. When the frequency of the sound equals that of the natural frequency of the canal then the sound is amplified, i.e. we have resonance.

3.2 Discomfort occurs because the pressures on either side of the eardrum are unequal. It can be reduced by rapid swallowing or by eating a sweet, which opens the auditory (Eustachian) tube and equalises the pressure in the middle ear.

3.3 Old intensity level = $10 \log_{10} \frac{10^{-4}}{10^{-12}}$ = 80 dB

New intensity level = $10 \log_{10} \frac{10^{-7}}{10^{-12}}$ = 50 dB

Thus the change in intensity level = −30 dB.

3.4 The patient's response to sounds both in air and applied to bone should be tested. In conductive deafness, in which the outer and/or middle ear is affected, the tests will show that air conduction is abnormal and bone conduction normal. If the problem lies in the inner ear, the hearing via both air and bone conduction will be abnormal.

End-of-chapter questions

1 The outer ear collects the sound. The key parts mentioned should include the pinna and the tympanic membrane. For the middle ear, the ossicles should be mentioned. Their role as levers together with the function of the Eustachian tube should be described. For the inner ear, the function of the organ of Corti should be explained.

2 a One type of deafness is conductive deafness, in which sound vibrations do not reach the inner ear. This could be due to wax in the outer ear or solidification of the bones in the middle ear, which may be corrected. A hearing aid would help.
Sensorineural deafness, in the inner ear, may only affect a small band of frequencies but cannot be cured by a hearing aid.

b Given that $I = 10^{-6}\,\mathrm{W\,m^{-2}}$ and $I_0 = 10^{-12}\,\mathrm{W\,m^{-2}}$ then the sound intensity level in dB
$= 10\log_{10}(I/I_0) = 60\,\mathrm{dB}$.

c Change in intensity level $= 10\log_{10}(I_2/I_1)$. But this is given as 15 dB, so
$10\log_{10}(I_2/I_1) = 15$
and
$\log_{10}(I_2/I_1) = 1.5$
Therefore the ratio of the new and old sound intensities is $10^{1.5} = 31.6$.

Chapter 4

Self-assessment questions

4.1 Equivalent dose = absorbed dose × quality factor (radiation weighting factor).
For the α-rays,
equivalent dose $= 20 \times 10 = 200\,\mu\mathrm{Sv}$.
For the γ-rays,
equivalent dose $= 1 \times 25 = 25\,\mu\mathrm{Sv}$.
Therefore the total equivalent dose $= 225\,\mu\mathrm{Sv}$.

4.2 Using the equation for effective dose and table 4.2, we get
effective dose $= 36 \times 0.12 + 11 \times 0.12 + 16 \times 0.05$
$+ 1 \times (0.2 + 0.12 \times 2$
$+ 0.05 \times 5 + 0.01 \times 2)$
$= 47 \times 0.12 + 0.8 + 0.71$
$= 7.15\,\mu\mathrm{Sv}$

4.3 a Radiation is absorbed by a photographic film which will blacken. The degree of blackening varies with the amount of radiation. Various types of radiation can be detected by the use of filters.

b The main disadvantage is that the amount of radiation cannot be measured until a reasonable time has elapsed.

4.4 Thermoluminescent devices are more accurate (and can record lower doses) but may be more expensive than the simple film badges. The badge is, however, a single-use device, whereas a thermoluminescent detector can be inspected whenever desired and reused a number of times.

End-of-chapter questions

1 The equivalent dose is 2.5 mSv from neutrons and 3 mSv from γ-rays. The total is 5.5 mSv.

2 The total equivalent dose is 15 mSv, which means that the radiation level is not exceeded.

Chapter 5

Self-assessment questions

5.1 X-rays produce good images when the target has a relatively high atomic number, Z, and/or relatively high density, for example bone rather than soft tissue.

5.2 A CT scan allows three-dimensional images to be recorded and displayed. Detail of organs deep in the body can be seen more clearly.

End-of-chapter question

A CT scan is desirable because it rapidly gives the precise location of a head injury. It also gives some information about the nature of the injury, but for a definitive diagnosis other clinical information is needed.

Chapter 6

Self-assessment questions

6.1 a It has a short half-life and emits only gamma rays.

b It can produce amounts of technetium-99m over a number of days, from which a number of patient doses can be prepared.

6.2 The right kidney must be functioning normally, since the activity against time graph increases initially and then decreases. In the left kidney the radiation increases continually showing that no urine, and hence no radiopharmaceutical, is being passed into the bladder.

6.3 **a** When ionising radiation interacts with a scintillator, light is emitted.

   b A collimator only allows the radiation that comes straight through the holes to be detected; it therefore defines the field of view. Fewer and larger holes give more sensitivity – i.e. a greater γ-ray detection level – but less definition.

End-of-chapter question

a Gamma radiation is used since it will pass out of the body without absorption.

b Six hours is a suitable half-life, since it allows measurements to be made but does not significantly cause problems to staff or the patient in terms of exposure to radiation. This is the half-life of technetium-99m.

Chapter 7

Self-assessment questions

7.1 The ratio is 0.000 921, which indicates that virtually all the ultrasound is transmitted through a muscle–soft tissue boundary.

7.2 B scans are used in pregnancy to measure safely, without any radiation dose, the size of the foetus (bi-parietal diameter or crown–rump length). Abnormalities can be diagnosed also.

7.3 **a** The Doppler effect is the apparent change in frequency of the sound emitted by a moving source. It can be used to measure the speed with which a reflecting interface moves.

   b The Doppler effect can be used to measure the blood flow rate in, for example, a heart, in order to check its functioning.

End-of-chapter questions

1 At the intensities used in medicine, ultrasound causes no damage to tissue. It operates by some of the ultrasound being reflected and some transmitted. It is used for examining soft tissue; it cannot pass through very dense tissue and is not useful for detecting bone damage.

2 At any boundary between two types of material (media), some ultrasound is reflected and some transmitted. The degree of reflection is determined by the acoustic impedances of the two media; acoustic impedance Z is density times sound velocity. At an air–skin boundary the Z-values are quite different, so ultrasound would be mostly reflected and little information would be received from within the body. If the space between ultrasound source and skin is filled with a gel that has a similar Z-value to skin, then most of the ultrasound will be transmitted through the gel–skin boundary, as required.

Chapter 8

Self-assessment question

8.1 **a** A hydrogen nucleus contains only one proton. Since this is an odd number, there is a net spin and so an NMR signal can be obtained.

   b A magnetic field orientates the hydrogen nuclei either along the field or in the opposite direction; the result is a very small excess in the field direction. A gradient field ensures that the total magnetic field is different at each point in the sample volume. Repeated RF pulses cause some nuclei to switch to the opposite alignment.

   c The relaxation times for the excited nuclei to disperse their energy can be deduced from the decay in amplitude of the RF signal emitted as they relax.

   d Different tissues can be distinguished by the difference in relaxation time. This difference comes about because if more water is present than in normal tissue, as is the case with cancerous tissue, the relaxation time (for both relaxation processes) is longer.

End-of-chapter question

a A static magnetic field allows the nuclei to align themselves in the direction of or opposite to the magnetic field; application of an RF field makes some nuclei change their orientation and gain energy. They subsequently give up this energy as an RF wave; this is then detected by a coil. The decay times (by two processes) of the signal are characteristic of the environment of the hydrogen nuclei.

b A very intense, steady, uniform magnetic field is used; superimposed is a very slight field gradient. There is an RF field which is switched on and then off.

c No ionising radiation is used, and there are no side effects at the intensities employed in MRI.

Chapter 9

Self-assessment questions

9.1 A treatment plan allows the required dose distribution of radiation in the body to be modelled in order to check that only tumour tissues will be destroyed. Isodose curves are lines joining points of equal radiation dose.

9.2 The accuracy of the beam is better with an accelerator than with a source. This reduces damage to healthy tissue.

9.3 At the outset it is possible that the source was not placed accurately, or it might move after being placed.

End-of-chapter question

A treatment plan is prepared from the diagnostic imaging information (X-ray, CT, NMR etc), to produce a plot of isodose lines for the particular case; the treatment machine's basic isodose lines have been modified to ensure that a cell-killing dose of radiation will be given to the tumour while sparing normal tissues. The treatment plan is checked using an X-ray simulator.

Depending on the type of tumour either external beams of radiation or sealed or unsealed internal sources may be used. Examples are given in the chapter.

Chapter 10

Self-assessment questions

10.1 **a** It avoids the need for an operation or permits the use of a very small incision. A cold light source is used, so no heat is delivered to the body.

b A coherent bundle of fibres allows an image to be returned from object to viewer while an incoherent bundle (which is cheaper) can be used to transmit light down the endoscope to illuminate the viewing area.

10.2 The light is of a single wavelength (only the wavelength that is needed) and the power density is high.

10.3 **a** Nd YAG, gallium arsenide and carbon dioxide.

b $\text{time} = \dfrac{\text{energy}}{\text{power}} = \dfrac{150}{20} = 7.5\,\text{s}$

End of chapter questions

1 No heat is generated inside the body. Clear images can be seen without major surgery. Tissue samples can be removed for examination.

There are two bundles of optical fibres, one to transmit light and the other to send an image back up. These need two different sets of fibres, incoherent and coherent respectively. The bundles of fibres are flexible and a camera can be attached to allow easy viewing.

2 **a** The laser is used to change the curvature by vaporising the excess tissue on the cornea. To change the shape a series of apertures is used.

b $E = P \times t = 20 \times 90 = 1800\,\text{J}$

Glossary

Absorbed dose the radiation energy absorbed per unit mass; measured in grays (Gy)

Accommodation altering the shape, and therefore the focal length, of the lens in order to focus on objects at different distances from the eye

Acoustic impedance the ability of a substance to refract ultrasound

Activity the number of radioactive disintegrations per second; measured in becquerels (Bq)

Astigmatism uneven curvature of the cornea

Audiometry testing for hearing loss

Blind spot the part of the retina from which the optic nerve arises, and where no rods or cones are present

Coherent fibres optic fibres which are arranged to have the same relative position at both ends of a bundle

Compton scattering an incident photon ejects an orbital electron from an atom, transferring only part of its energy to the electron. The photon, now with reduced energy, moves off in an altered direction.

Conductive deafness hearing loss caused by damage to the conduction process within the outer and middle ear

Cone a receptor cell in the retina of the eye; there are three types each receptive to a different range of wavelengths of light, so providing colour vision

Cornea the curved, transparent tissue at the front of the eye that is responsible for most of the refraction of light as it enters the eye

Decibel (dB) unit of noise level

Depth of field the range of distances over which objects are in focus

Doppler effect the change in observed frequency of reflected radiation when an object moves away or towards an observer

Equivalent dose absorbed dose × quality factor

Effective dose Equivalent (now called Effective dose) takes account of dose equivalent and different organs of the body. The sum of product of organ weighting factor and equivalent dose for each organ irradiated.

Far point the furthest distance at which the eye can focus

Gray (Gy) unit of absorbed dose. $1 \, \text{Gy} = 1 \, \text{J} \, \text{kg}^{-1}$

Hypermetropia (long sight) an eye defect in which distant objects are in focus but close objects are blurred

Intensity level power per unit area

Isodose curves lines joining points of equal radiation dosage

Joint the connection between two or more bones where some degree of movement is usually permitted

Ligament a band of tissue that holds together the bones of a joint

Linear accelerator a radiotherapy machine which produces a high energy electron beam. It can be used to treat surface cancers, but is more usually fired onto a tungsten target to produce a high energy X-ray beam to treat deeper tumours.

Loudness a subjective response to an intensity of sound

MRI Magnetic Resonance Imaging

Myopia (short sight) an eye defect in which near objects are in focus but distant objects are blurred

Near point the nearest distance at which the eye can focus

Optic nerve the nerve which transmits optical signals to the brain

Pair production an X-ray photon interacts with the nucleus to produce an electron positron pair

Photochemotherapy treatment of certain skin diseases using light

Photoelectric effect an incident photon ejects an orbital electron from an atom, transferring all of its energy to the electron

Photopic vision vision which occurs with cones to detect different colours

Power of a lens the focussing power of a lens. Measured in dioptres (D)

Presbyopia the deterioration in the ability of the eye to accommodate as we get older

Radiopharmaceutical the combination of pharmaceutical (determining distribution of complex within the body) and a radionuclide. For diagnosis, gamma emitters are used.

Retina the layer of cells at the back of the eye that is sensitive to light

Rod a receptor cell in the retina of the eye that is sensitive to relatively dim light, but not to colour

Scintillator material which, on absorption of radiation, emits a flash of light

Scotopic vision vision which uses rods to detect light levels. Mainly used in night vision.

Sensorineural deafness deafness due to problems in the inner ear or in the auditory nerve pathway

Sievert (Sv) the unit of equivalent radiation dose and effective radiation dose

Tendon a strong strand of tissue which attaches muscle to bone

Threshold of hearing the minimum intensity audible at a given frequency

Transducer a device for transferring energy between different systems

Ultrasound frequencies of sound above the threshold of human hearing (≈ 20000 Hz). Medical ultrasound usually operates at frequencies of a few MHz.

Yellow spot the point on the retina at which there is a high concentration of cone cells and at which detailed vision is best

Index

Terms shown in **bold** also appear in the glossary (see pages 86–7). Pages in *italics* refer to figures.